SENSUOUS
PESSIMISM

SENSUOUS PESSIMISM

Italy in the Work of
Henry James

Carl Maves

INDIANA UNIVERSITY PRESS
Bloomington / London

Published in Canada by Fitzhenry & Whiteside Limited,
Don Mills, Ontario

Library of Congress catalog card number: 72–75640
ISBN: 0–253–35177–4

MANUFACTURED IN THE UNITED STATES OF AMERICA

To Ian Watt,

Che porta il lume dietro, e sè non giova,
Ma dopo sè fa le persone dotte

CONTENTS

FOREWORD

Ian Watt

"I am not a topographical writer." Thus Conrad, peremptorily declining an invitation to immortalize the vales of Kent, so long his home. Henry James was a topographical writer, and in the simplest sense: like any other self-respecting nineteenth-century novelist he occasionally turned out travel books. It goes without saying that they were of a special kind. *Portraits of Places* and *Italian Hours*, not to mention *The American Scene*, assume we've already traveled beyond Baedeker; that we ask, not what we ought to see, but what special human meanings reside in what we have seen.

In fiction this is the question which the regional novelist typically attempts to answer: Hardy and Giono and Faulkner are spiritual ecologists; the major premise both of their lives and of their works is the territorial imperative; and their novels reveal how particular habitats determine human histories. But Henry James was obviously not a regional novelist, and was an ecologist only in the sense that, as in his life he belonged to, so in his fiction he mainly portrayed a small but prosperous and growing group of international vagrants. For them, place had no coercive force, and they located themselves (and their books) wherever best satisfied their own private hopes and wishes. So we might say of James's novels that they are written in the mood, not of the territorial imperative, but of the ecological subjunctive.

James was a vagrant almost from birth; and his travels soon led him to follow in the steps of a whole host of Northern writers, from Goethe, Shelley, and Byron to Hawthorne, Browning, and

Ibsen, for whom Italy had been the predestined other place. Italy's appeal to James was immediate and total. On his first visit to Rome he announced to his brother: "At last—for the first time—I live." From then on James confessed himself "the life-long victim" of "the most beautiful country of the world," the "subtlest daughter of History."

How deeply and continuously Italy figures in James's fiction is Carl Maves's main theme. His aim is essentially different from those of such earlier studies as Van Wyck Brooks's *The Dream of Arcadia: American Wrtiers and Artists in Italy, 1760–1915*, or Nathalia Wright's *American Novelists in Italy; The Discoverers: Allston to James.* Maves's study goes beyond social history and literary tradition to seek just what Henry James can have meant when he wrote that for him Rome was "a rare state of the imagination."

Like the dream, the imagination has its own particular geography. Sometimes its places do not exist on the map, like Shakespeare's Bohemia; sometimes they only appear to, like Hamlet's Denmark; and sometimes they are real places which have been transformed into literary clichés. Among cities Paris is the prime example of this last, as James realized. In his first notes for *The Ambassadors*, for example, he worried about "the banal side" of making Paris the setting for Strether's revelations. "It might be London—it might be Italy" James reflected, before being forced to the regretful conclusion: "I'm afraid it must be Paris, if he's an American."

Henry James's imaginative geography of Italy was somewhat similar to E. M. Forster's. Both men had actually lived more in France, and knew it better; in Italy they were essentially tourists —informed, loving and frequent, no doubt, but still tourists. But it was Italy, not France, which they chose in their novels to stand for the polar opposite to their own native ways of life, to Sawston or to the northeastern seaboard of the United States. There were, of course, profound differences in the way they saw the opposition. On one hand James certainly found it more difficult than Forster to endorse some of the human values which Italy has traditionally represented to the Northern literary imagination— notably the unrestrained public enactment of the emotions and appetites. On the other hand James gave a much greater role to the Italian past. Here it was presumably his own literary needs which were decisive. Much more than Forster's, James's pastel-crowded palette needed blacks as well as reds and golds; and in his novels the dark residues of history serve, not merely as local color, but as reminders of intractable realities which lie in wait for vagrants who stay too long; it is in Rome that Isabel Archer must accept her suffering, because Rome is the imagination's capital city for intrigue, betrayal, and decay.

James's first exercise on the international theme, "Travelling Companions" in 1869, was also his first story with an Italian setting. From then on James's imaginative geography of Italy develops in resonance and complexity through such early masterpieces as *Portrait of a Lady* and *The Princess Casamassima* until it arrives at the two great finales of *The Wings of the Dove* and *The Golden Bowl.* It was in this last, as Maves writes, that James created his only European character who is "depicted from the inside." Prince Amerigo is, as he tells Maggie in a momentous scene, in part a mere epitome of Italy, of "the history, the doings, the marriages, the crimes, the boundless bêtises of other people." Yet the Prince aspires to be more than the sum of his place and his past; there is also, he affirms, "another part, smaller doubtless, which such as it is, represents my single self, the unknown, unimportant save to you—personal quality."

Maves finely comments: "The Prince, in short, aspires to modernity, he wants to throw off history and become an individual." The enterprise, much more difficult for an American than he is likely to assume, is all but impossible for an Italian; yet out of the struggle a sense of selfhood can arise which is less vulnerable to the coercions of place and time than the selfhood of those who have not been so long and deeply exposed to these intractable imperatives. One surmises that the Prince's sad lucidity, which, as Maves writes, is "constantly alert to the abyss of irony that yawns beneath all human endeavor," was essential not only to the Prince's achieved selfhood, but, more generally, to the pitiless burden of meaning with which Italy finally outstared Henry James. At least, it is only in Italy that the imagination of the Master discovered, in the Prince but also in Gloriani and Eugenio, a command of experience so absolute that James seems to have felt both envious and intimidated.

The passage, incidentally, has a curiously prophetic quality; for, as yet another century lurches toward its close, the continuing infatuation of America for Europe is still liable to be suddenly transformed into a sense of outraged betrayal by the slightest sign that ungrateful Europe may be contemplating throwing off the yoke of its history, and trying to be itself.

This is only one of the remoter general perspectives suggested by a book which offers abundant rewards to the reader; most abundantly no doubt to those readers who, like myself, cannot too often pay "the old, the familiar tax on the luxury of loving Italy"—and Henry James.

ACKNOWLEDGMENTS

Like the "relations" Henry James mentions in the Preface to *Roderick Hudson,* proper acknowledgments "stop nowhere," and the "exquisite problem" of the scrupulous author is "to draw, by a geometry of his own, the circle within which they shall happily *appear* to do so." My own geometry must necessarily exclude many important Jamesian critics not cited below whom I have nevertheless frequently consulted; and it can only appear to include all personal debts consciously incurred during the gestation of the present work.

It is therefore right to begin with Professor Henry Terrie of Dartmouth College, who first cultivated my interest in James and has never ceased to nourish it over more than a decade of friendship. I am similarly grateful to Professor Ian Watt, who took hold of this book when it was a mere mewling dissertation project at Stanford University and helped immensely in bringing it to some semblance of manhood.

For permission to quote unpublished correspondence between James and the Waldo Story family I am obliged to the generosity of the Humanities Research Center Library of the University of Texas at Austin, where Mrs. Sally Leach was of special assistance, and to Professor Leon Edel and Mr. Alexander James, who holds the copyright on that material.

This study has further benefited from acute comments on the manuscript by Professor Terrie and by Professors J. A. Ward and Walter Isle of Rice University, and from the bounteous encouragement of Mrs. Dorothy Wikelund of Indiana University Press. It was more obliquely fortified by the kindnesses of various colleagues at Dartmouth College and Southern Methodist University; by my typist Mrs. Carol Naab; and by Professor Carl Spring of the University of California at Davis, who provided me a most pleasant environment for revision and second thoughts. That is not really all, of course; but it is perhaps enough.

Dallas, February 1972

CHRONOLOGY

The following chart schematizes the connection between Henry James's various Italian sojourns—fourteen separate visits over a period of 38 years—and the major works discussed below. Though James spent, in all, little more than four years of his life in Italy, this relatively small total is evidence of a phenomenon he himself often noted: the disparity between the duration of an experience and its importance to the creative temperament.

HENRY JAMES IN ITALY *(some dates are necessarily approximate)*	HENRY JAMES ON ITALY *(unless noted, all dates are of first publication)*
7 Sept. 1869—14 Jan. 1870	"Travelling Companions" (1870); "At Isella" (1871)
26 Aug.—10 Sept. 1872	"The Madonna of the Future" (1873)
23 Dec. 1872—10 June 1873	"The Last of the Valerii"; "Adina" (1874)
10 Oct. 1873—20 June 1874	*Roderick Hudson; Transatlantic Sketches* (1875)
20 Oct.—12 Dec. 1877	"Italy Revisited" (1877); "Daisy Miller" (1878); "The Diary of a Man of Fifty" (1879)

26 March—30 May 1880; 26 Feb.—2 July 1881	*The Portrait of a Lady* (1881); *Partial Portraits* (1884); *The Princess Casamassima* (1886)
5 Dec. 1886—15 July 1887	"The Aspern Papers" (1888); "The Solution" (1889)
Several days in Nov. 1888; 14 May—10 Sept. 1890; 5 June— 5 Aug. 1892; 24 March—5 July 1894	"The Grand Canal" (1892)
5 April—7 July 1899	"Two Old Houses and Three Young Women" (written 1899); "Miss Gunton of Poughkeepsie" (1900); *The Ambassadors* (written 1901); *The Wings of the Dove* (1902); *William Wetmore Story and His Friends* (1903); *The Golden Bowl* (1904)
20 May—26 June 1907	"The Velvet Glove"; *Italian Hours* (1909)

SENSUOUS
PESSIMISM

Prologue
1869

I

"I am thinking a little of Italy," Henry James wrote from Switzerland to his friend John La Farge on June 20th, 1869.[1] James was twenty-six and had not yet been south of the Alps; he crossed them soon afterwards, however, and was destined to think a great deal about Italy for the rest of his life. "Of all the countries of Europe," says Morton Dauwen Zabel, "Italy excited in James the strongest romantic feeling, the most intense sensuous emotion and perhaps the richest evocations to be found in his essays and tales."[2] Examining just how and why this is so may illuminate a large and important segment of the Jamesian canon.

One reason for Italy's special appeal to James is that he discovered it absolutely on his own. In all the protracted European wanderings of his childhood the James family never once touched there, and Henry's initial Italian pilgrimage was thus made alone, as a mature young man with fourteen published short stories to his credit. The effect on him was profound; he later remarked that "the world has nothing better to offer to a man of sensibility than a first visit to Italy during those years of life when perception is at its keenest, when discretion has arrived, and yet youth has not departed." [3] Italy then had for him a uniquely personal meaning; his involvement with it—or with "her," as he would have said—had somewhat the intensity of a love affair. As Leon Edel points out, "in the writings about it the word 'passion' crops up at every turn, in letter, in travel impression, in story." [4]

To be sure James did not capitulate all at once, though from the beginning he found Italy "unspeakably fair and interesting." Venice was his first big impression: "quite the Venice of one's dreams," he called it,

> but it remains strangely the Venice of dreams more than of any appreciable reality. The mind is bothered with a constant sense of the exceptional character of the city; you can't quite reconcile it with common civilization. It's awfully sad, too, in its inexorable decay.[5]

Similarly in Florence he found a "perfect felicity of picturesqueness"; [6] but it was Rome that finally overwhelmed him. The letter to his brother William commemorating this occasion reads like the account of an ecstatic conversion:

> At last—for the first time—I live! It beats everything: it leaves the Rome of your fancy—your education—nowhere. It makes Venice—Florence—Oxford—London—seem like little cities of pasteboard. I went reeling and moaning thro' the streets, in a fever of enjoyment. I traversed the whole of Rome and got a glimpse of everything. . . . The effect is something indescribable. For the first time I know what the picturesque is.

And he concludes: "In fine I've seen Rome, and I shall go to bed a wiser man than I last rose." [7] The emotion thus evoked proved permanent; but over a period of forty years, up to *Italian Hours* in 1909, James continually refined its expression.

Still, the emotion was not completely spontaneous. There were precedents for James's specific reaction that were a part of his "fancy" and "education": the year before his first visit he could already speak of Italy, in a review of William Dean Howells's *Italian Journeys,* as "a deeply interesting country" endowed with "a sort of half-sacred character." [8] He inherited that oddly persistent Anglo-Saxon conception of it, dating at least from the Renaissance, which on the one hand sees Italy as a venerable relic of the Roman Empire, as purveyor and exemplar of culture and civilization, a land of carefree sensuous enjoyment and sunny skies inhabited by "simple and natural folks, pleased . . . with little things, and as easy and unconscious as children in their ways," [9] while on the other hand viewing it, like Roger Ascham in *The Scholemaster* (1570), as the sink of elegant vice and luxurious corruption, of subtle treachery with dagger and poison, of cynical sensual indulgence and Machiavellian casuistry, a moral hothouse pullulating with Jesuits, assassins, and courtesans.

In literature the latter viewpoint is perhaps the more conspicuous, being highly visible from *The White Devil* to Shelley's *The Cenci* and after; its alternative attained new prominence in the Romantic era with Goethe's *Italienische Reise,* Madame de Staël's popular novel *Corinne,* and the voluminous attitudinizings of Lord Byron, who proclaimed Italy "the garden of the world, the home/Of all Art yields, and Nature can decree." [10] Italy was subsequently celebrated by such eminent Victorians as the Brownings and Ruskin, and America too contributed its individual note. There was not only the example of Hawthorne to draw on: since the early nineteenth century, colonies of American artists had flourished in Florence and especially in Rome, where young Henry James often enjoyed the hospitality of the sculptor William Wetmore Story, a Boston expatriate and close friend of the Brownings.[11] And on his first visit to Italy James added a fresh influence to that of *The Marble Faun* and *Modern Painters:* he carried around a copy of *La Chartreuse de Parme,* whose author he found "a capital observer and a good deal of a thinker." [12] Stendhal's novel, as we shall see, affected James's ideas on Italy perhaps more than any other single work.

II

The focus of this study is the precise nature of James's response to Italy, primarily as shown in his fiction. There is no attempt to catalogue every reference to the subject in his work; the approach utilized here is not exhaustive and merely descriptive but selective and interpretive.[13] James's writings about Italy show a remarkable continuity. From the start they are dominated by three general motifs or broad thematic areas which recur and intertwine, developing complexly while retaining their identities. For convenience these may be summarily labeled the motifs of romance, of treachery, and of sensuousness.

The first of these partially derives from the circumstances under which James first toured Italy. In 1869 the goals of the Risorgimento had yet to be realized: Rome was still ruled by the Pope and the rest of the peninsula was largely under foreign control. By the time of James's second visit in 1872, however, the Republic had been established and the old picturesqueness, many travelers felt, was gone forever. "It seems to me," Howells lamented in *Italian Journeys,* "that all moisture of romance and adventure has been well nigh sucked out of travel in Italy," and it is certainly demonstrable that James himself began to feel nostalgic for what Italy had lost rather early in their acquaintance.[14] Yet the motif's main foundation is doubtless the romantic image of Italy that James indulgently cherished and that the real Italy could scarcely live up to on every occasion. The young visitor in fact became immediately cognizant of the split between the sentimental pre-conceptions of the *forestieri* and the harsh practical Italy of the Italians themselves; he saw how most Americans tended to ideal-ize Italy, a tendency he further saw as closely related to the American innocence that he so shrewdly chronicled. While alert to such falsifications, however, he found it personally impossible all his life to think of Italy without to some extent romanticizing it, and he often utilized this Janus-like awareness in his fiction.

It is but a short step from an Italy that arouses unreal expecta-tions to an Italy that actively deceives, and thus arises the second motif, treachery. Howells sighs over "the unfathomable, dis-heartening duplicity of the race," and in a letter dated October 13, 1869, James himself calls the Italians "false and beautiful": [15] his fiction first imagines them cynically catering to the romantic prejudices of Americans and later, by a curious sort of transfer-ence, makes Italy a specialized setting for conspiracies and be-trayals carried on wholly by Anglo-American visitors. Frequently in such stories American innocence and its penchant for idealiz-ing are subtly exploited by these visitors, thus establishing a further interconnection between motifs. Treachery within close personal relationships is at the basis of much Jamesian fiction, and in most cases it is perpetrated against an Italian background.

But if Italians are "false" they are also "beautiful"—James indeed finds that the combined beauty of its people, landscape, and art makes Italy irresistibly attractive, even though this total appeal to the senses dizzies his moral equilibrium by inevitably entailing a glorification of the carnal at the expense of the spiritual. He quickly comes to view the Italians as deeply expert in the life of the flesh, as "embodiments of feeling, without intel-lectual complications . . . in whom expression is immediate and complete," which means among other things that they exemplify for him, particularly the men, the power of the sexual instinct.[16]

Measured against the artifice of romance and deceit, sex, at least, is a reality, but James found it difficult to treat fictionally, and only in his last major novel does Italian sensuousness emerge as the equal of the other two motifs.

The Golden Bowl also provides a convenient touchstone for the special intensity of James's "Italian emotion." There is finally something mysterious and obsessive about it: Italy represents possibilities that he can never fully accept or define and never long ignore. The novel's Italian Prince lives with his American wife in England, where the even tenor of his life is occasionally interrupted by

> a low music that, outside one of the windows of the sleeping house, disturbed his rest at night. Timid as it was, and plaintive, he yet couldn't close his eyes for it, and when finally, rising on tiptoe, he had looked out, he had recognized in the figure below with a mandolin, all duskily draped in her grace, the raised appealing eyes and the one irresistible voice of the ever-to-be-loved Italy. Sooner or later, that way, one had to listen; it was a hovering, haunting ghost, as of a creature to whom one had done a wrong, a dim pathetic shade crying out to be comforted.[17]

The Prince here fashions his homesick yearnings into an allegory that recalls James's own nostalgia for romantic Italy. He too, an American living in England, was thus haunted: he heard the same appeal for nearly half a century, he was another who "had to listen."

2

A Moral Holiday
1870-1873

I

Henry James returned from Europe to Cambridge in May 1870; though nostalgic for Italy, he resumed literary labors immediately.[1] In the next three years he wrote five tales with Italian settings, tales which this chapter will investigate at length, first, because they set forth nearly all the specifically Italian elements in James's fiction, and second, because though of considerable interest, they have rarely been scrutinized closely on any basis.

The *Atlantic Monthly* for November and December 1870 published James's first truly international story, "Travelling Companions." Two earlier tales, indeed, had European settings: "A Tragedy of Error" (1864) and "Gabrielle de Bergerac" (1869). But they are melodramas with French casts and scenery, whereas the later work, which is set in Italy, marks James's initial attempt to depict Americans abroad; it clearly adumbrates the international theme that would shortly come to dominate his fiction, and eventually, with "Daisy Miller" (1878), bring him widespread recognition and success.

"Travelling Companions" itself, however, is a comparatively primitive effort. "Its trivial action," says one critic, "is merely the thread on which James strings his own responses to Europe," and he certainly seems to have composed it much in the manner of the Hawthorne who transferred long descriptive passages from his Italian notebooks into *The Marble Faun* with only minor adjustments.[2] The result of such a procedure is more a travelogue than a work of fiction: the simple narrative—Mr. Brooke meets Miss Evans in Milan, courts her in Venice, and, after her father's death, marries her in Rome—is largely overshadowed by extended elaborate set pieces on Da Vinci's *Last Supper,* Verona and Padua, St. Mark's basilica, and the Roman Campagna. Though the dialogue is clever enough, characterization is minimal. The two lovers are conventionally high-minded and little else, and only the father, a blunt, hearty retired businessman, is sufficiently differentiated to attain the vividness even of caricature.

"Travelling Companions" thus finds its closest analogue in the sort of Technicolor film that stitches together exotic locales with a thin romantic fable; it is the scenery that counts, people are only a pretext. The distance between author and narrator is often so infinitesimal as hardly to be calculable; if the plot is obviously fictional, detail after detail is pure autobiography. Brooke announces, for example, that "this is my first visit to Italy," [3] and walks around "with a volume of Stendhal in my pocket" (185), doubtless *La Chartreuse de Parme.* Yet the story finally distinguishes itself from the lavish expenditures of sensibility in the letters by presenting a concentrated, coherent attitude toward Italy that is almost completely independent of the narrative and that clearly provides the basis for much of James's subsequent fiction, however tentatively or crudely expressed here.[4] To be sure, there is nothing systematic about this attitude; on the contrary, the response to Italy is turbulently emotional, eloquently expounded rather than analyzed. Brooke says early on that "I had dreamed of this Italian pilgrimage, and . . . had at last undertaken it in a spirit of fervent devotion" (175). He finds that Italy "exhaled the pure essence of romance" (184); later Miss Evans tells him that "all this Italian beauty and delight has thrown you into a romantic state of mind" (203).

Romance, romantic; these are important words, the more so because they are difficult to define. In his preface to *The American* James views romance as characterized by "disconnected and uncontrolled experience," [5] and for the James of "Travelling Companions" the romantic emotion is seemingly that which reduces the life around it to discrete aesthetic phenomena. Brooke speaks of "Northern Italian towns" which are

> shabby, deserted, dreary, decayed, unclean. In those August days the southern sun poured into them with a fierceness which might have seemed fatal to any lurking shadow of picturesque mystery. But taking them as cruel time had made them and left them, I found in them an immeasurable instruction and charm.

Here squalor is termed "picturesque," another key word in a story throughout which Italy is intensely *seen* rather than comprehended. "Wherever I turned," says Brooke, "I found a vital principle of grace—from the smile of a chambermaid to the curve of an arch" (185); the romantic bias perceives only the beautiful, and the beautiful is always visual.

At times, significantly, the purely romantic and sensuous responses to Italy heighten into the sensual and even the downright sexual. Words like "desire" and "passion" spatter the page recurrently; Brooke says of his arrival in Venice:

> The day succeeding . . . I spent in a restless fever of curiosity and delight, now lost in the sensuous ease of my gondola, now lingering in charmed devotion before a canvas of Tintoretto or Paul Vero-

nese. I exhausted three gondoliers and saw all Venice in a passionate fury and haste. I wished to probe its fullness and learn at once the best—or the worst. (191–2)

Most startling of all is Brooke's fervid metaphor on the view from the Milan cathedral:

This prospect offers a great emotion to the Northern traveller. A vague, delicious impulse of conquest stirs in his heart. From his dizzy vantage-point, as he looks down at her, beautiful, historic, exposed, he embraces the whole land in the far-reaching range of his desire. (179)

The implication here is not merely of invasion, but of intercourse: James's traveler is a modern-day Vandal literally lusting after the South.

But this overwhelming voluptuousness inexorably brings on its post-coital opposite, and again and again in "Travelling Companions," romantic delight is succeeded by romantic sorrow. Thus the Byronic Brooke claims that in Italy "at every step I gathered some lingering testimony to the exquisite vanity of ambition" (185), and in Giotto's chapel at Padua he notes "an irresistible pathos in such a combination of shabbiness and beauty" (210). In most cases this is perhaps mere melancholy of the Childe Harold variety, though at times there is a genuine and troubled recognition of the disparity between aesthetic response and the misfortune it often preys on, of the inappropriateness of the romantic emotion as applied to what would normally be considered private or painful or disgusting. After being accosted by a mysterious stranger in the Milan cathedral, Brooke tells Charlotte Evans: "This poor woman is the genius of the Picturesque. She shows us the essential misery that lies behind it. It's not an unwholesome lesson to receive at the outset" (183). In St. Mark's, however, he experiences his most typical revulsion of feeling: "To this builded sepulchre of trembling hope and dread, this monument of mighty passions, I had wandered in search of pictorial effects. Oh vulgarity!" But he immediately adds, "of course I remained, nevertheless, still curious of effects" (193). Such guilt feelings can only be transient; in romantic Italy, the ethical confounds itself with the pictorial until the two are inextricable.

Yet such reactions—the reveling in Italian sensuousness, the resultant pangs of conscience—are, after all, those of a foreigner, and specifically of a Protestant Anglo-American temperament confronted for the first time with the alien South, with a Catholic, Mediterranean, basically hedonistic world that seems not simply opposed, but indifferent, to Puritan and Calvinistic values. As James Russell Lowell said, Italy offers us "a sense of freedom from responsibility," [6] a holiday from morality, a suspension of the rules one usually judges by, a respite from the rigorous in favor of the relaxed; and the offer can be alternately viewed as delectable or deeply dangerous, as the fruit of edenic innocence or the wisdom of the serpent. In "Travelling Companions" James has it both ways. Brooke as a newcomer to Italy appreciates Milan for its "temperate gayety—the softness of the South without its laxity" (181), yet a page later he exhorts Charlotte Evans:

> We must forget all our cares and duties and sorrows. We must go in for the beautiful. Think of this great trap for the sunbeams, in this city of yellows and russets and crimsons, of liquid vowels and glancing smiles being, like one of our Northern cathedrals, a temple to Morality and Conscience. It doesn't belong to heaven, but to earth—to love and light and pleasure. (182)

And in Naples he measures the ethical distance he has traveled since entering Italy: "As I looked upward at Northern Italy, it seemed, in contrast, a cold, dark hyperborean clime, a land of order, conscience, and virtue" (220).

Sometimes, indeed, a balance between the moral and the pleasurable seems almost possible: comparing Tintoretto's *Cruci-fixion* with the "deified human flesh" of his *Bacchus and Ariadne,* Charlotte Evans asks in wonder, "What do you think . . . of the great painter of darkness being also the great painter of light?" (207).[7] But in general the sense of threat, of imminent or latent evil, is never wholly vanquished. In St. Mark's, for instance, Brooke suddenly feels that "the great mosaic images, hideous, grotesque, inhuman, glimmered like the cruel spectres of early superstitions and terrors" (193). This Puritan bias, this suspicion in the midst of aesthetic delight, clearly affects Brooke's sternest judgment of all, on the Italian people themselves. They are, he decides, beautiful, talented, charming; they excel at "the unapplied, spontaneous moral life of society" (185); but they lack moral force, they are too facile, too nonchalant, too passive in the toils of fate. The crucial passage occurs in Venice at Florian's. Brooke and Miss Evans are watching some "young Venetian gentlemen" seated nearby:

> They sat rolling their dark eyes and kissing their white hands at passing friends, with smiles that were like the moonflashes on the Adriatic.
> "They are beautiful exceedingly," said Miss Evans; "the most beautiful creatures in the world, except—"
> "Except, you mean, this other gentleman."

Whereupon they shift their attention to a party of "genuine Anglo-Saxons" dominated by a "young man" whose face

> was full of decision and spirit; his whole figure had been moulded by action, tempered by effort. He looked simple and keen, upright, downright.
> "Is he English?" asked Miss Evans, "or American?"

"He is both," I said, "or either. He is made of that precious clay
that is common to the whole English-speaking race." (196)

Such crude stereotyping is a sign of acute discomfort on James's
part; he feels obligated to judge and yet unable at this point to
judge on his own.

Offensive though this incident may be, however, it indicates
the terms on which the "international theme" becomes a measurable force in the guidebook world of "Travelling Companions."
That force is never great, but the raw material is at least presented and its potential indicated. It may initially seem odd that
James's American narrator is made an expatriate—"I have been
living in Germany" (174), he tells the heroine's father, "by education I am a German"—but the strategy soon becomes evident:
Brooke is meant to function as a sympathetic yet detached observer of Americans abroad, close enough for involvement with
them but distant enough for careful evaluation of their foibles.
He himself explains:

> Americans had come to have for me, in a large degree, the interest
> of novelty and remoteness. Of the charm of American women, in
> especial, I had formed a very high estimate, and I was more than
> ready to be led captive by the far-famed graces of their frankness
> and freedom.

Thus at his first encounter with Charlotte Evans, Brooke senses
"a different quality of womanhood from any that I had recently
known; a keenness, a maturity of conscience, which deeply stirred
my curiosity. It was positive, not negative maidenhood" (178).
Similarly, when he meets her in Venice he feels "more even than
before that she was an example of woman active, not of woman
passive" (194). Charlotte Evans is as demonstrably Anglo-Saxon
as the blond young man at Florian's, but she is also something
more, an independent, unconventional American girl whose ac-

tions Brooke ponders with somewhat the interest that Winterbourne is later to expend on Daisy Miller.

The analogy is strengthened when Brooke recalls "that young American ladies may not improperly detach themselves on occasion from the parental side" (176): later he meets Miss Evans unescorted in the streets of Venice and is "lost in wonder. . . . I had heard of American girls doing such things; but I had yet to see them done" (205). Her father is momentarily called away; she and Brooke visit Padua together, miss the train back, and are obliged to spend the night there. Miss Evans does not seem unduly upset, and yet, says the expatriate, "I was unable to detach myself from my Old World associations. . . . The miserable words rose to my lips, 'Is she Compromised?' If she were, of course, as far as I was concerned, there was but one possible sequel to our situation" (212). The next day he dutifully proposes marriage, and is told: "you imagine that I have suffered an injury. . . . I don't believe in such injuries" (217). As Mr. Evans explains, "My daughter is a d——d proud woman!" (216). If Charlotte Evans is proud, Brooke is, in his own opinion, strangely diffident and aloof. Like Stendhal's Fabrice he agonizes over whether or not he is in love and at one point admits, "I felt that I was not possessed by a passion; perhaps I was incapable of passion" (214). Although the protagonists of "Companions" finally do marry, their relationship is a genteel, embryonic version of what, eight years later in "Daisy Miller," will become a vivid clash of opposites.

What is after all most vivid in "Travelling Companions," however, is the tourism: the sensuous impact of Italy, the aesthetic enthusiasm, the romantic welter of James's responses to his surroundings. Fittingly enough, perhaps the story's most memorable incident deals with a fictional work of art. In Vicenza Brooke is approached by a young man who "might have been a young prince in disguise, a Haroun-al-Raschid" (187). Immediately we enter the world of Hawthornean romance: the young man has a mother and invalid sister to support; taking Brooke home, he offers for sale a family heirloom, "a most divine little Correggio" Madonna, whose face, Brooke discovers, "bore a singular resemblance to that of Miss Evans . . . . The young American rose up in my mind with irresistible vividness and grace. How she seemed to glow with strength, freedom, and joy, beside this sombre, fading, Southern sister!" (188-9). The girl tells him she has dreamt of a stranger who

> kneeled down before the little Madonna and worshipped her. We left him at his devotions and went away. When we came back the candles on the altar were out: the Madonna was gone, too; but in its place there burned a bright pure light. It was a purse of gold! (190)

Brooke buys the painting, and thinking of the Vicenza family on his way to Venice, is filled "with a painful, indefinable sadness. So beautiful they all were, so civil, so charming, and yet so mendacious and miserable!" (191). The judgment obviously has wider applications, and so has the incident as a whole. The connection of image with actuality, the contrast between the two young women, the dream: surely the total effect is that of allegory. The American woman is the new Madonna, the Old World is wasting away and the New World must restore it; Italy offers Americans art, while America can offer Italy only gold—all this is implied and more, so delicate are the reverberations of the episode. Quaint though it may be, James is in control here as nowhere else in the story; we feel that if real works of art stimulate rhapsody, fictional works of art prompt artistry.

Allegory makes yet a further appearance in "Travelling Companions." On the last page the reunited lovers stand before Titian's *Sacred and Profane Love* and Brooke explains that "The serious, steady woman is the likeness, one may say, of love as an experience—the gracious, impudent goddess of love as a sentiment; this of the passion that fancies, the other of the passion that knows" (225). This startlingly idiosyncratic passage has implications far beyond its original context.[8] Such a balancing of "sentiment" and "experience," of "the passion that fancies" and "the passion that knows," of imagination and intellect, schematizes perhaps the major tension in James's own mind, a tension that Italy seems to have first reduced to its elemental terms: shall we be passively sensuous or actively analytic, shall we view life romantically or realistically, should we yield to its surface charms or probe beneath for unifying values? This particular conflict colors the international theme as a whole but is most vividly apparent in the fiction about Italy and Italians; it thus forms an essential strand in the Jamesian carpet and one that can be profitably traced throughout this study.

In the meantime, though there is obviously more "sentiment" than connected and controlled "experience" in the love affair with Italy that "Travelling Companions" celebrates, the potentials for development are solid indeed. James even seems cognizant of a possible reconciliation between Sacred and Profane Love: confronted with the splendor of "the South in nature, in man, in manners" (181), Brooke exults that "for the first time I really *felt* my intellect" (175); "my perception," he says, "seemed for the first time to live a sturdy creative life of its own" (184).[9] Italy, then, does not merely drug the senses or provoke the critical faculties; rather, in some way James has yet to investigate fully, it effects that combination of feeling and intellect, of perception and passion, without which a great novelist is impossible—and Italy unfathomable.

II

James's second Italian tale, "At Isella" (1871), is, like "Travelling Companions," a fictionalized travelogue, but this time there is no attempt to disguise the fact: the first third of the piece is entirely travel reminiscence and what remains is pure story. This seeming technical regression has a curious counterpart in subject matter, for "At Isella" opens with a young American in Switzerland eagerly anticipating his first visit to Italy, and it is at the point he crosses the border that the guidebook becomes fiction.

The narrator, who is never named, nurses a febrile impatience to see Italy all the while he is laboriously describing Swiss scenery, since as he puts it, "What was Switzerland after all? Little else but brute nature surely, of which at home we have enough and to spare. What we seek in Europe is Nature refined and transmuted to art." [10] Once he has decided to join "the ranks of southward-trooping pilgrims" (308), little else interests him besides "premonitions of Italy"; he presses onward, toward where "tomorrow and Italy seemed merged in a vague bright identity" (310). Finally he reaches "the Italian slope of the Simplon road" and ecstatically breathes "Italian air"; he stops at an *osteria* "devotedly to quaff a glass of sour wine to Italy gained," and exults that "I had gained my desire"—though he has not even passed through customs, which in itself proves a major experience:

> At last, at a turn in the road, I glimpsed the first houses of a shallow village, pressed against the mountain wall. It was Italy—the Dogana Isella! so I quickened my jaded steps. I met a young officer strolling along the road in sky-blue trousers, with a moustache *à la* Victor Emanuel, puffing a cigarette, and yawning with the sensuous ennui of Isella. . . . A few steps more brought me to the Dogana, and to my first glimpse of those massive and shadowy arcades so delightfully native to the South. Here it was my privilege to hear for the

first time the music of an Italian throat vibrate upon Italian air. "Nothing to declare—niente?" asked the dark-eyed functionary, emerging from the arcade. "Niente" seemed to me delicious; I would have told a fib for the sake of repeating the word. (318–19)

The rapturous emotion in the above passages verges on the comic; indeed, only the charm of the details and the general air of naiveté keep encroaching bathos at a distance. Nowhere else does the special intensity of James's feeling for Italy so utterly overwhelm him. The prose swoons, everything is charged with the same significance and is significant merely because it is Italian, the usually discriminating consciousness renders homage without irony or discrimination.

The narrator, in short, is at Isella; and suddenly the travelogue vanishes, the tourist becomes a person, and the story begins. He puts up at the local inn, and as he proceeds to order dinner, the host announces: "I shall take the liberty . . . of causing monsieur to be served at the same time with a lady" (319). This news renders him "indefinably curious, expectant, impatient. Here was Italy at last; but what next? . . . I had been deeply moved, but I was primed for a deeper emotion still" (320). He glimpses the mysterious, agitated lady out for a walk; the host muses over her situation in a speech palpitant with sexual innuendo. "Of what romance of Italy was she the heroine?" (322) wonders our hero— and dinner is served.

We are back, then, in the world of "romance," of the glamor that foreigners impose on Italy with the "mendacious" coopera- tion of its inhabitants. Bruce McElderry explains that in "At Isella" the American narrator "identifies himself with romantic Europe by helping a beautiful Italian lady escape to Switzerland to join her lover." [11] As a statement of the narrator's own viewpoint this is accurate enough, though James certainly suggests that much of the romance in the story derives from his hero's imaginative need for it. The above-mentioned dinner, for instance, demonstrably begins on a faint note of the bogus: "As I installed myself," says the young man,

> opposite my companion, after having greeted her and received a murmured response, it seemed to me that I was sitting down to one of those factitious repasts which are served upon the French stage, when the table has been moved close to the footlights, and the ravishing young widow and the romantic young artist begin to manipulate the very *nodus* of the comedy. Was the Signora a widow? (323)

Still further on, we are told that the lady "shrugged her shoulders —an operation she performed more gracefully than any woman I ever saw, unless it be Mlle Madeleine Brohan of the Theatre Français" (326); and this same teasing fragrance of theatricalism eventually saturates the story to an extent perhaps that James did not even intend.

The narrator, in any case, is utterly convinced of the lady's "candid passion," and proceeds to make her an extraordinary avowal:

> "I have come on a pilgrimage," I said. "To understand what I mean, you must have lived, as I have lived, in a land beyond the seas, barren of romance and grace. This Italy of yours, on whose threshold I stand, is the home of history, of beauty, of the arts—of all that makes life splendid and sweet. Italy, for us dull strangers, is a magic word. We cross ourselves when we pronounce it. We are brought up to think that when we have earned leisure and rest—at some bright hour, when fortune smiles—we may go forth and cross oceans and mountains and see on Italian soil the primal substance— the Platonic 'idea'—of our consoling dreams and our richest fancies. . . . Here I sit for the first time in the enchanted air in which love and faith and art and knowledge are warranted to become deeper passions than in my own chilly clime. I begin to behold the promise

of my dreams. It's Italy. How can I tell you what that means to one of us? (327–8)

The emotion here is specifically religious in its ardor and abandon; yet the narrator with his "fancies" and "dreams" also tacitly rejects what James in "Travelling Companions" called Sacred Love and opts instead for the Profane. It is clearly implied that the lady may feel free to wield her influence however she wishes on so absolute an enthusiast: "Ever since I could use my wits . . . I have done little else than fancy dramas and romances and love-tales, and lodge them in Italy. You seem to me as the heroine of all my stories" (328). There is in these words a covert plea for deception, or at least for some sort of transcendance of the boundary that usually separates romance from reality. The young American wants passionately to enter the fiction he has already created for himself out of "the Platonic idea" of Italy.

We must subsequently wonder to what degree the lady consciously complies with his prejudice and works his susceptibility. At least she is well aware of it. At one point he tells her he is to meet his fiancée in Florence and compares the position of unattached women in Italy and America:

> "Fewer things are 'supposed' of women there than here. They live more in the broad daylight of life. They make their own law."
> "They must be very good then—or very bad. So that a man of fancy like you, with a taste for romance, has to come to poor Italy, where he can suppose at leisure!" (330)

The lady, obviously, is rather less of a romantic herself: " 'The Charm of Italy!' cried the Signora, with a slightly cynical laugh. 'Foreigners have a great deal to say about it' " (326).

But by this time the narrator has promised to help the Signora in any way he can, and soon after she obligingly supplies the details he craves. She is fleeing from a brutal husband to her lover who lies ill in Geneva, she fears being overtaken, she lacks the money for a private carriage. It is a lurid tale of anguished flight and noble desperation, and the young American is understandably dazzled:

> I listened with a kind of awe to this torrent of passionate confidence. . . . Her tale, in a measure, might be untrue or imperfect; but her passion, her haste, her sincerity, were imperiously real. . . . My heart beat fast; I was part and parcel of a romance. Come! the dénouement shouldn't fail by any prosy fault of mine. (335–6)

Among "prosy" faults the narrator presumably numbers skepticism, scrupulous regard for the truth, and a concern for the proprieties involved; nothing has importance beyond his determined assumption of the role not simply of participant in a romance, but of the artist who will bring it to a satisfactory conclusion. He impulsively empties his billfold; the lady seizes the money "with both her hands"; minutes later the carriage is ready and she leaves the inn "as if she had equally forgotten my face and her obligations." He muses that "my hour was over" but cannot resist a last confrontation: the lady asks for his blessing and tells him succinctly, "Love is selfish, Signore." So she departs, and the narrator is left "a wiser, possibly a sadder man than a couple of hours before. I had entered Italy, I had tasted of sentiment, I had assisted at a drama. It was a good beginning" (336–8). He dreams tumultuously that night, and is awakened by the arrival of the husband, whom the host, as instructed, fends off with a lie; and thus the story ends.

Are we to think that the lady has lied too, that the narrator has been the willing victim of a fabrication? To such an inquiry, however, "At Isella" is completely opaque. There is no way to determine how much of the Signora's plea is calculated deception and how much is truth, or even whether or not James means us to doubt her much at all, for he consistently refuses to judge his Italian characters by ordinary ethical standards; this is as true of the Signora as it will be of the Prince Amerigo in *The Golden Bowl.* But it is at least clear that the narrator has found the consummation he lusted after on the story's very first page: "Nature refined and transmuted to art." His experience with the lady is ersatz only by "Northern" standards; in Italy, life is inseparable from drama, from romance.[12] Like the story itself, the narrator, in entering Italy, passes from fact to fiction, and to that state of mind, dangerous and irresistible both, where existence is judged and valued, not for its moral worth or intrinsic truth, but solely for its glamor and intensity.

III

The Cambridge exile ended in May 1872 when James once again sailed for Europe. Of course he visited Italy, and his second tour there directly furnished the material for the two essays reprinted in *Transatlantic Sketches* (1875) as "From Chambéry to Milan" and "From Venice to Strasburg."

What is most notable in the first sketch is the distinct lessening of moral tension as James once again enters Italy. In Chambéry he visits Les Charmettes, the house where Rousseau and Madame de Warens lived together. It is haunted, he reflects, "by ghosts unclean and forlorn. The place tells of poverty, trouble, and impurity." [13] Yet ten pages later this same "stern moralist," finally safe on Italian ground, can lightly banter his reader about an excursion to Lake Como,

> which, though brief, lasted long enough to make me feel as if I too were a hero of romance, with leisure for a love affair, and not a hurrying tourist, with a Bradshaw in his pocket. The Lake of Como has figured largely in novels with a tendency to immorality—being

commonly the spot to which inflammatory young gentlemen invite the wives of other gentlemen to fly with them and ignore the restrictions of public opinion.

Situations taken seriously in Switzerland are astonishingly less serious in Italy. The reason why is provided a few sentences later when James wonders where he has "seen it all before," meaning the scenery at Lake Como, and answers himself:

> Where, indeed, but at the Opera, when the manager has been more than usually regardless of expense? Here, in the foreground, was the palace of the nefarious barytone, with its banqueting-hall opening as freely on the stage as a railway buffet on the platform; beyond, the delightful back-scene, with its operatic gamut of coloring; in the middle, the scarlet-sashed *barcaiuoli,* grouped like a chorus, hat in hand, awaiting the conductor's signal. It was better even than being in a novel—this being in a libretto. (83–4)

Here, as in "At Isella," Italy figures as theater and Italian life as theatrical, and both are to be judged by aesthetic rather than ethical standards.[14] One does not condemn the theater for depicting immorality but rather for depicting it badly, inartistically, and in Italy it is depicted very artistically indeed.

A similarly "romantic" attitude is expressed in the second essay, where James, on a visit to Torcello, near Venice, is beset by urchins clamoring for alms:

> They were very nearly as naked as savages, and their little bellies protruded like those of infant Abyssinians in the illustrations of books of travel; but as they scampered and sprawled in the soft, thick grass, grinning like suddenly translated cherubs, and showing their hungry little teeth, they suggested forcibly that the best assurance of happiness in this world is to be found in the maximum of innocence and the minimum of wealth. (88–9)

This is a disquieting passage: we sense something animalistic and terrifying about the children and something innocent in James's attributing to them "the maximum of innocence." How unsophisticated really can he suppose such children to have been? Surely his own aesthetic bias has misled him here, just as the narrator of "At Isella" was misled by the lady's glamorous plausibility. James is not yet fully attuned to the presence of contemporary as opposed to historical evil in the Italy he loves; his very next piece of fiction, however, shows an increasing awareness of it.

IV

Written in Paris toward the end of 1872, "The Madonna of the Future" is one of James's most successful early tales; [15] it extends his view of Italy as artifice by depicting for the first time an artist in Italy, though Theobald could more precisely be called an artist *manqué.* An expatriate American and longtime resident of Florence—which James had not yet revisited and perforce remembers from 1869—he has never sold a painting, chiefly because he has never painted one. What prevents him is his desire to create a perfect Madonna, the modern equivalent of Raphael; thus for twenty years he has been priming himself to undertake a masterpiece by contemplating the beauty of an Italian woman, Serafina. Finally, however, a friend, the first person to whom he has ever introduced the woman, frankly tells him that he has waited too long—she is too old for a Madonna. Theobald's illusion is shattered; realizing the utter futility of his endeavor, of his life, he sinks into despair and dies.

The story's title, then, is ironic, as is its portrayal of the gap between the ideal and the actual, a gap which James makes all the more vivid by detaching the subject of the narrative, Theobald, from the person who narrates it, an unnamed young New Yorker on his first visit to Florence. In "Travelling Companions" and "At Isella" narrator and protagonist are one, and the resultant gush of subjectivity swamps the story, while the tone of perfervid enthusiasm leaves little room for nuance. Now, though, we have a sympathetic observer who can gather his impressions disinterestedly and give us Theobald in a light he himself could not furnish, and the gain is immense; the focus sharpens, the prose is more pointed. Theobald, for instance, delivers a diatribe reminiscent of the hero's passionate avowal in "At Isella," but this time an alternate view is provided:

> "We are the disinherited of Art!" he cried. "We are condemned to be superficial! We are excluded from the magic circle. The soil of American perception is a poor little barren, artificial deposit. . . . We poor aspirants must live in perpetual exile."
> "You seem fairly at home in exile," I answered, "and Florence seems to me a very pretty Siberia. But do you know my own thought? Nothing is so idle as to talk about our want of nutritive soil, of opportunity, of inspiration, and all the rest of it. The worthy part is to do something fine! There's no law in our glorious Constitution against that." [16]

One attitude challenges another here, but neither is allowed to triumph; James seems to want tension, not resolution.

This new ironic lucidity extends even to details. Theobald, having presented the narrator to Serafina, leaves them alone for a moment:

> When he arose to light the candles, she looked across at me with a quick, intelligent smile and tapped her forehead with her forefinger; then, as from a sudden feeling of compassionate loyalty to poor Theobald, I preserved a blank face, she gave a little shrug. (33)

A few pages later Theobald is asked if the Madonna will ever be painted: " 'I'll finish it,' he cried, 'in a month! No, in a fortnight! After all, I have it *here!*' And he tapped his forehead" (38). Serafina thinks he is mad, Theobald himself thinks he is a genius;

the story's truth resides in the balance of extremes maintained by its central intelligence.

And from any viewpoint "Madonna" is a study in extremes, the extremes of Theobald and Serafina, idealism and pragmatism, art as religion and art as commerce, American innocence and Italian sophistication. In "Travelling Companions" and "At Isella" a haze of romanticism was equally diffused over every person and object; in "The Madonna of the Future" the haze is for the most part only in Theobald's mind, and the world outside it, the real world, appears harsh and sordid by contrast. Whether primarily an effect of the detached narrator or not, there is now a definite polarization between how Italy is seen by the foreigner and what Italy and Italians really are. James is more critical, more willing to know rather than just fancy; the relationship of passionate pilgrim to the idol he worships becomes explicitly one of victim and victimizer.

It is doubtless true, one must add, that Theobald in many ways qualifies as his own worst enemy, debilitated as he is by an idealism that seems the terminal stage of the romantic agony, romanticism refined to a theory and completely detached from action. The less committed romantic, like Brooke of "Travelling Companions" or James himself in 1869, unthinkingly steeps everything he sees in the colors of aesthetic emotion; an idealist like Theobald consciously heightens the emotion into a religion by seeking absolute forms behind the apparent, by intellectualizing the picturesque instead of simply yielding to it. Thus he regularly employs the rhetoric of conversion, asceticism, fanaticism:

> One by one, all profane desires, all mere worldly aims, have dropped away from me, and left me nothing but . . . the worship of the pure masters . . . . My little studio has never been profaned by superficial, feverish, mercenary work. It's a temple of labor, but of leisure. (16)

Standing before the *Madonna della Seggiola* he specifically articulates his credo: Raphael's genius is supreme because

> No lovely human outline could charm it to vulgar fact. He saw the fair form made perfect; he rose to the vision without tremor. . . . That's what they call idealism; the word's vastly abused, but the thing is good. It's my own creed, at any rate. Lovely Madonna, model at once and muse, I call you to witness that I too am an idealist! (20-21)[17]

The narrator realizes Theobald's sincerity but also his limitations. Though the painter burns with a "high aesthetic fever," he is, as a matter of "vulgar fact," utterly alienated from aesthetic reality. He has verbalized plastic art until it has become a matter more of *poesis* than of *pictura,* has abstracted it completely from the world it supposedly depicts, has, in short, exalted Profane Love and called it Sacred—a significant confusion as opposed to the reconciliation that James himself envisaged in one of the travel essays of 1872, when he noted that the paintings of Tintoretto resolve "the eternal problem of the conflict between idealism and realism. . . . I defy the keenest critic to say where one begins and the other ends. The homeliest prose melts into the most ethereal poetry, and the literal and imaginative fairly confound their identity." [18] Here is precisely the synthesis Theobald is incapable of; for him the connection between the ideal and the actual had been substantially lost. The result is sterility: he is artistically paralyzed, he cannot create, can only comtemplate a pastiche, a *"resumé* of all the other Madonnas of the Italian school" (28).

His most egregious folly is, of course, his self-deception regarding Serafina, who after twenty years is still for him "the most beautiful woman in Italy" (30). The narrator, however, sees "an elderly woman. She was neither haggard nor worn nor gray; she was simply coarse" (33). He tries to dissipate his friend's "illusion," his "charmed inaction," but Theobald can only ask, "If she is old, what am I? . . . Has life been a dream?" (37). The actual has finally overtaken the ideal, and the idealist is shattered by the force of the encounter.

But the remainder of the story makes it clear that Theobald is not solely responsible for his delusion. Serafina herself has tacitly fostered it with the ultimate excuse that if his life was a dream, at least his dream was a life. In this she is akin to the Vicenza family of "Travelling Companions" and the Signora in "At Isella": they are all part of the Italy that, with the utmost good-natured calculation, furnishes romance to order. If the *forestieri* from America want illusion, these indigenes are perfectly willing and more than able to provide it—for a price. They can see, furthermore, no compelling reasons, moral or otherwise, for drawing a strict line between the real and the fabricated; in a land of flamboyant theatricalism such distinctions are often impossible to make anyway.

Thus when the narrator, in search of the ailing Theobald, discovers the middle-aged Madonna very much *en famille* with a mustachioed artisan, she is chagrined—James describes her "sinister flush"—but by no means remorseful. She believes Theobald's mind has been "poisoned . . . against her," and warns, "It would be no kindness to the poor gentleman, I can tell you that." Despite what his friend may think, she has not taken advantage of Theobald, but rather protected him:

> The world has so little kindness for such persons. It laughs at them, and despises them, and cheats them. He is too good for this wicked life! It's his fancy that he finds a little Paradise in my poor apartment. If he thinks so, how can I help it?

And she concludes with the essence of her philosophy: "In this hard world one mustn't ask too many questions; one must take what comes and keep what one gets" (41–2). This is pragmatism of the narrowest sort—cynical, amoral, opportunistic—but there is also the implication of an attitude more clearly stated in Serafina's words to the narrator after Theobald's death:

> It was a pity he ever brought you to see me! Of course, you couldn't think of me as he did. Well, the Lord gave him, the Lord has taken him. I've just paid for a nine days' mass for his soul. And I can tell you this, Signore, I never deceived him. Who put it into his head that I was made to live on holy thoughts and fine phrases? It was his own fancy, and it pleased him to think so. (51)

Serafina's hard-headed practicality, then, is pervaded by a fatalistic acceptance of the world she must live in. If illusion is gratifying, why dispel it? Pleasure in life is scarce enough.[19]

It is ironic that Serafina, for all her crassness, is perfectly right about Theobald: without his sustaining illusions, he inevitably perishes of having "taken it all too hard"; given the extremes of the story, it is only artists like Serafina's mustachioed lover that flourish. The latter produces satiric statuettes, animals that caricature people. The narrator examines his wares:

> They consisted each of a cat and a monkey, . . . and illustrated chiefly the different phases of what, in delicate terms, may be called gallantry and coquetry; but they were strikingly clever and expressive, and were at once very perfect cats and monkeys and very natural men and women. I confess, however, that they failed to amuse me. I was doubtless not in a mood to enjoy them, for they seemed to me peculiarly cynical and vulgar. Their imitative felicity was revolting. (44)

These figurines fall just short of pornography, as their sculptor himself points out: "I have been free, but not too free—eh? Just a hint, you know! You may see as much or as little as you please"

(45). A note of sexual nausea is unmistakable in this episode, which implies the aesthetic opposite of Theobald's idealism, human characteristics debased instead of exalted, reduced to their lowest animalistic level.[20] Once again synthesis fails; there is no middle ground here between Theobald's impotence and the sculptor's prurient facility, though the dying painter glimpses the possibility of one: "I'm the half of a genius! Where in the wide world is my other half? Lodged perhaps in the vulgar soul, the cunning, ready fingers of some dull copyist or some trivial artisan who turns out by the dozen his easy prodigies of touch!" (48). At last he realizes what he needed all along: a touch of the practicality that Italy might have taught him, but which instead was used to foster his delusion.

"The Madonna of the Future," then, moves beyond "Travelling Companions" and "At Isella" to conclude that it is not just foolish, but even dangerous, to idealize Italy and Art—the two at this point are nearly synonymous. A healthy involvement with either seems to demand some combination of the romantic and the real which remains as yet hypothetical, though at least James is beginning to show us that life in Italy is not enthralling only because it is more dreamlike but also because it is more substantial than life elsewhere. It prepares one for extremes, for the carnal in human experience as well as the spiritual, and hopefully for the two mixed and inseparable: this particular service is reaffirmed in the very last words of the story. Once Theobald is buried the narrator leaves Florence to brood elsewhere on his own experience:

> For a week afterwards, whenever I was seized among the ruins of triumphant Rome with some peculiarly poignant memory of Theobald's transcendent illusions and deplorable failure, I seemed to hear a fantastic, impertinent murmur, "Cats and monkeys, monkeys and cats; all human life is there!" (52)

V

On December 18, 1872, James left Paris to winter in Rome, where he arrived, after a three year absence, on the 23rd. He remained until June 1873, and was later to think of these days as among the happiest in his life. The travel articles he continued to write for American periodicals provide direct impressions of his sojourn; there are five on Rome in *Transatlantic Sketches,* or over a quarter of the book.

The word "picturesque" abounds on every page; churches, landscapes and local color are described profusely and charmingly. James's enthusiasm is scarcely contained—his surroundings so totally delight him that he seems to gloss over all complexities in his haste to enjoy. How can the "childishness" of the Roman people be "intimately connected with Roman amenity, urbanity, and general gracefulness"? [21] James does not pause for analysis, but rushes on to find riding on the Campagna a "supremely irresponsible pleasure" because the scenery there is "so bright and yet so sad, so still and yet so charged, to the supersensuous ear, with the murmur of an extinguished life" (136–7). As usual, the shadow of romantic guilt sometimes darkens his enjoyment. "To delight in the evidence of meager lives might seem to be a heartless pastime, and the pleasure, I confess, is a pensive one" (148), he muses, and says of Genzano that "the tourist can hardly help wondering whether the picture is not half spoiled by all that it suggests of the hardness of human life" (161). But his instinct for the "supersensuous" always reasserts itself, and when spring comes he waxes positively voluptuous: "Nature surrenders herself to it with a frankness which outstrips your most unutterable longings" (183). No wonder he concludes that "the Roman atmosphere is distinctly demoralizing" (199).

VI

Despite his supposed enervation, however, James wrote at least two tales during his Roman holiday, the first of which was "The Last of the Valerii." Its narrator is once again a detached observer, in this case a leisured elderly American who paints genre scenes. His goddaughter Martha marries a young Italian nobleman, Camillo Conte Valerio: this is the first of James's international marriages and has immense interest as a prototype. Martha supplies the alliance with Yankee dollars; the Count's contribution, besides his beautiful person, is a Roman villa of venerable antiquity that his bride wishes to reclaim from decay. At her urging systematic excavations are begun on the grounds, in the course of which a magnificent image of Juno is uncovered.[22] The Count's reaction to the find, however, exceeds mere admiration. He starts neglecting Martha to spend all his hours with Juno, and finally worships the statue in exhausting vigils and blood sacrifice. His unhappy wife, brought to realize the source of her trouble, orders the Juno reinterred, whereupon the Count, free of his marble succubus, takes Martha back in his arms and resumes his marriage.

A curious tale, and old-fashionedly "romantic" too. Leon Edel calls Count Valerio "a kind of sleepy, dreamy, well-fed Donatello," [23] and certainly one seems to hear the creak of Hawthorne's supernatural-allegorical machinery in the background. American purity confronts Old World "evil," a statue exerts sinister power on the heir of a tainted race: perhaps it is right to note here some regression, something of a backward glance, in James's art. Still, Hawthorne's treatment of Rome in *The Marble Faun* was not only a conspicuous precedent but an unavoidable influence. The younger author had not yet rethought the city on his own terms, and given a common American bias, many of his first impressions naturally coincided with those of a literary predecessor, who, after all, claimed to know Rome "better than my birth place." [24] But Rome made a further difference: it moved James to deal specifically with that element of the Italian heritage and consciousness stemming not just from Renaissance or medieval times, but from the even more removed pre-Christian era of Empire and fabulous power, of strange gods and cruel customs. It is an alien element, a dangerous element; such at least is the opinion of the narrator, who in a moment of depression sees the Count as

> a dark efflorescence of the evil germs which history had implanted in his line. . . . The unholy passions of his forefathers stirred blindly in his untaught nature and clamored dumbly for an issue. What a heavy heritage it seemed to me, as I reckoned it up in my melancholy musings, the Count's interminable ancestry! [25]

The story then is basically about Camillo Conte Valerio and how the dark ancestral past impinges on his tranquil modern existence. The Count commands our attention throughout and is the only character treated in any detail; "The Last of the Valerii" thus represents James's first important piece of fiction to center on a European. Camillo is initially presented to us as an amiable, very handsome, rather stolid young man. The narrator speaks of his "heavy sincerity" and describes "a head as massively round as that of the familiar bust of the Emperor Caracalla, and covered with the same dense sculptural crop of curls." Like Prince Amerigo in *The Golden Bowl,* the Count more than once gives the impression of an expensive artifact: "His complexion was of a deep glowing brown which no emotion would alter, and his large lucid eyes seemed to stare at you like a pair of polished agates" (89–90).[26]

The intellect of this gorgeous object is quite another matter. "He was perhaps a little stupid," we are told on the first page, and later the godfather bursts out in exasperation that the Count seems

> fundamentally unfurnished with "ideas." He had no beliefs nor hopes nor fears—nothing but senses, appetites, and serenely luxurious tastes. As I watched him strolling about looking at his fingernails, I often wondered whether he had anything that could properly be termed a soul, and whether good health and good-nature were not the sum of his advantages.

The narrator goes on to doubt that Camillo can further Martha's "moral development": "What was becoming of her spiritual life in this interminable heathenish honeymoon?" (95–6). Spiritual values have, in truth, little place in the Count's life. When Martha speaks of converting before their marriage, he advises her to "keep your religion. . . . Every one his own. If you should attempt to embrace mine, I'm afraid you would close your arms about a shadow. I'm a poor Catholic" (93). Camillo may be a "poor Catholic," but he is a "good Italian"; if he is not at all religious, he is, again like Amerigo, strongly superstitious. He expresses a distaste for the plans to excavate at Villa Valerio, and when twitted about it replies:

> Yes, by Bacchus, I am superstitious! . . . Too much so, perhaps. But I'm an old Italian, and you must take me as you find me. There have been things seen and done here which leave strange influences behind! . . . Don't dig any more, or I won't answer for my wits! (98–9)

And this as it turns out is the fairest of warnings. Camillo dreams on the day of the discovery that "they'd found a Juno; and that she rose and came and laid her marble hand on mine" (101); he proves unable to break the grip. It is here that the story approaches and perhaps enters the realm of the occult; but the Count's worship of the statue is carefully left open to rational interpretation. The narrator is sure he himself understands what has happened: he meditates on "the strange ineffaceability of race-characteristics" (111) and says of Camillo to his goddaughter: "He has reverted to the faith of his fathers. Dormant through the ages, that imperious statue has silently aroused it. . . . In a word, dear child, Camillo is a pagan!" (116).

The explanation offered here is one of simple atavism: the Count is a throwback to a far-distant pagan era, or at least part of him is:

> The poor fellow has but half succumbed: the other part protests. The modern man is shut out in the darkness with his incomparable wife. . . .[27] He has proved himself one of the Valerii; we shall see to it that he is the last, and yet that his decease shall leave the Conte Camillo in excellent health. (117)

Such is the thrust of the story's title; and the implication of "we shall see to it" is that Camillo alone lacks the strength, moral or intellectual, to resist effectively. Though his face wears "an expression which I fancied was not that of wholly unprotesting devotion" (114), leading the narrator to suppose that "the Juno was becoming daily a harder mistress to serve" (116), the Count by himself is helpless; it takes a plucky wife to save the situation by deciding that the Juno is "beautiful, she's noble, she's precious, but she must go back!" (120).

Camillo then from one point of view is a pawn of "urgent ancestry" salvaged by American enterprise, and on these grounds one may find the story either inanely chauvinistic or charmingly Gothic, but in any case probably not very credible psychologically. There is, however, another dimension to the Count's malaise. The statue is, after all, a great work of art, "an embodiment of celestial supremacy and repose" (91), and some of his response to it derives from its solely aesthetic powers. When he begins avoiding his wife's company to worship Juno, the narrator comments: "That he should admire a marble goddess was no reason for his despising mankind; yet he really seemed to be making invidious comparisons between us" (106). The statue rouses, for the first time in his life, Camillo's dormant intellect—he sees how a bust of Hermes "suggests the most delightful images" (108), and at one point the narrator envies him "the force of his imagination" (113)—but it also unfits him for the exigencies of an imperfect world; the vision of absolute beauty has paralyzed him, rendered him disfunctional, even as it did Theobald in "The Madonna of the Future." The one ceases entirely to paint, the other neglects his role as husband; both are deluded, neither has any control over his delusion. Furthermore, in each case the usual categories of the actual and the ideal are reversed. Theobald sees Serafina only as his perfect Madonna,, and the Contessa laments, "His Juno's the reality; I'm the fiction" (117). Art creates its own romantic reality, a reality that sustains Theobald until its dispersal kills him. The Count, however, survives handily, in part because of his Italian resilience, but mostly because his romanticism, unlike Theobald's, is instinctive rather than voluntary; his *amour propre* can emerge unimpaired since his behavior from the outset has been ethically neutral.

These two stories thus resemble each other in yet another way: both deal with specifically Italian wrongdoing, and in both, despite the evidence, Italians plead not guilty. Once again a moral holiday is decreed: Serafina's fatalism goes far to mitigate her exploitation of Theobald, certainly in her eyes and possibly in ours too, and the Count's superstitious fears, his atavistic tendencies, real or supposed, completely excuse him from responsibility for the neglect of his wife. Everything reprehensible in Italy and in Italians, these stories seem to say, can be blamed on the horrors of the past or the inevitable harshness of existence—it is never the result of a human action consciously willed. Camillo impresses us as essentially passive from the beginning; in the course of the story he makes no decisions but instead yields himself to events; at the end, after his ordeal, he is unchanged and simply reverts to his former passivity. Someone remarks of the Juno, "the Count treats her as if she were a sacrosanct image of the Madonna" (105), and Camillo's reconciliation with his wife is described thus: "he strode forward, fell on his two knees and buried his head in her lap" (122). The gesture combines worship and an appeal to the maternal; Camillo in effect trades one Madonna, one Juno, one image, for another. Admittedly the trade is to his advantage; but the heritage of the Valerii, and of Italy in general, has not after all been expunged.

VII

The second of James's Roman tales is "Adina," the simple story of how Sam Scrope, an unpleasant young American classicist, cheats the handsome and naive Angelo Beati out of a disinterred relic, which after cleaning proves to be a priceless engraved topaz from the age of Tiberius. Scrope subsequently becomes engaged to his lovely stepcousin Adina Waddington, whereupon the vengeful Angelo, having been denied reparation for his loss, surreptitiously diverts the girl's affections and elopes with her; in a fit of pique Scrope flings "the baleful topaz" [28] into the Tiber.

The story has much in common with "The Madonna of the Future" and "The Last of the Valerii." All three use a detached observer as narrator; in "Adina" he is a "mild, meditative" friend of Scrope's. In each of them one of the major characters is an

Italian valued primarily for aesthetic qualities; the first time we see Angelo he is called "statuesque." In each of them a work of art—Theobald's presumptive Madonna, the Juno, the topaz—not only influences the action but precipitates it, generally with dire results. Yet as literature "Adina" is considerably less effective than the other two, mainly because the observer in this case is much too detached from the events he narrates. We never understand exactly how Adina is strange, nor why she runs off with Angelo; we never see their courtship either directly or indirectly, since the narrator is not in their confidence. This shortcoming unfortunately deadens the total impact of a story which nevertheless has several interesting aspects.

Scrope, for instance, represents a new type in James's fiction about Italy. Up to now his touring Americans have consistently tended to be dazzled by it; even bluff, no-nonsense Mr. Evans in "Travelling Companions" finds life there quite pleasant enough. Scrope in contrast is determinedly antiromantic and doggedly unimpressed by Italian splendor. He is described as "irreverent" and "caustic," fond of pretending "that he enjoyed nothing, and that what sentimental travellers call picturesqueness was a weariness to his spirit" (211). He scoffs at his friend's enthusiastic idealism as "absurdly Byronic" and "used to swear that Italy . . . was a land of vagabonds and declaimers . . . that nothing grew strong there but lying and cheating, laziness, beggary and vermin." Scrope's opinions clearly partake of the Protestant ethic and Puritan moralism, of a background basically unimaginative and ascetic. But there is also a more personal reason for his dour outlook:

> The truth was that the picturesque of Italy, both in man and in nature, fretted him, depressed him strangely. . . . To appreciate the bitterness of this dumb disrelish of the Italian atmosphere, you must remember how very ugly the poor fellow was. (212–13)

To Scrope, in other words, the Italian ubiquity of beauty is both a challenge and an affront; this explains why a man in general so rigidly "honest" can coldly bilk poor Angelo of his priceless discovery. He rationalizes his action at length, but the narrator understands better:

> his meager faculty of pleasing . . . prompted him now to regale himself, once for all, with the sense of an advantage wrested, if not by fair means, then by foul, from some sentient form of irritating Italian felicity. (221)

But this covert envy also renders Scrope's behavior immensely tortuous. At one and the same time he puts himself and Angelo in opposing moral categories and denies Angelo the right to judge him morally:

> The young fellow gave a strange smile.
> "Have *you* a good conscience?" he demanded.
> "Hang your impudence!" cried Scrope, very red.
> "What's my conscience to you?" (219)

The narrator is right to see him as "the victim of a moral hallucination" (235): Scrope is in the miserable position of needing to justify, logically and ethically, an action whose essential nature was passionate and unscrupulous. Like Theobald he attempts to invest his "hallucination" with a judicious solidity, to indulge Profane Love as if it were Sacred; but unlike Theobald he does so coldly and arrogantly. Scrope in fact represents, as we shall see, the first of James's corrupted expatriate Americans, and he also demonstrates himself in many ways the exact antithesis of James's characteristic Italian. He is ugly rather than beautiful, impervious to sensuous appeal, a desperate sophist rather than an easy amoralist. "Rigid Sam Scrope" (220), the narrator calls him, and toward the end of the story feels an "increase of pity for my friend's want of pliance" (247). It is precisely the pliancy of Italian life that James proposes to show us in these first Italian stories.

Angelo at least is flexible enough to take Adina when he cannot have the intaglio, and even finally to prefer what she offers: "She's better than the topaz" (256). He is, indeed, James's initial attempt to portray character development in an Italian. When Scrope and the narrator first come across him dozing on the Campagna and awaken him, he is a "young Roman clodhopper" with "something very simple—a trifle silly—in his smile" (214–15).[29] Scrope calls him "an idiot" and a "giggling lout"; offered ten *scudi* for the topaz, he can only make the American "a dumb appeal to his fairness" (219). The narrator meets Angelo next on Christmas day in the Colosseum, future scene of other important Jamesian encounters.[30] The young Italian has realized in the interim what a "fool" and "donkey" he has been: he looks "three years older . . . graver, manlier, and very much less rustic" (229). It is not just his appearance that is "greatly altered"; the narrator sees something more significant:

> it seemed to me that he had parted with something more precious even than his imperial intaglio. He had lost his boyish ignorance— that pastoral peace of mind which had suffered him to doze there so gracefully with his head among the flowers. (233)

Note that James says "ignorance," not innocence. Perhaps we are meant to infer that Angelo has become complex but not corrupt. He seems in his maturity to be directly modeled on Stendhal's Fabrice: both young heroes are somberly reflective, passionate without violence, and basically gentle.

In any case, though Angelo swears that "I shall think only of my revenge!" (233), he is curiously slow to act, whereupon the narrator supposes him to be restrained by "that saving grain of discretion which mingles with all Italian passion" (235). Later on, however, he mentions Angelo's "romantic ineffectiveness," and notes in the Italian's face "no evil . . . and no malignity, but a deep, insistent, natural desire which seemed to be slumbering for the time in a mysterious prevision of success." There is a definite hint here of that passive fatalism James seems to find so typical of the Italian temperament, a hint supported by Angelo's conviction that "the Lord does with us as he pleases" (243); but the most obvious explanation of Angelo's "deep, insistent, natural desire" is Adina. By now he has met her, though they have been alone only briefly. Angelo nevertheless maintains that "she understood me . . . such as it was she understood" (238), and we are left to imagine the basis of their understanding. It must be that Adina feels an immediate attraction, sexual or romantic or both, for the handsome Italian, since their elopement is accomplished in remarkably short order.[31] "Good-bye to everything! Think me crazy if you will. I could never explain" (253), says Adina's farewell note, and at this point James apparently could not explain either.

He makes an indirect attempt at it, however, when the narrator visits the young couple and finds Angelo "looking quite the proper hero of his romance." Reproaches seem somehow inappropriate:

> I was no more disposed than I had been a week before, to call him a bad fellow; but he was a mystery—his character was as great an enigma as the method of his courtship. That he was in love I don't pretend to say; but I think he had already forgotten how his happiness had come to him, and that he was basking in a sort of primitive, natural, sensuous delight in being adored. It was like the warm sunshine, or like plenty of good wine. . . . He was welcome to all his grotesque superstitions, but what sort of a future did they promise for Adina? (255)

We never know. Angelo has become a figure of amoral and time-
less carnality, a fact of nature; Adina herself wishes "to utterly
forget her past" and in turn "to be forgotten." As the story ends
the two components of this odd international marriage merge
into oblivion and the "mystery" of Italian sensuality, and that
mystery is, in the final account, all that "Adina" leaves us with.
There is, certainly, some effort made to equip the topaz with a
"curse," but such pseudo-Hawthornean gloom seems forced and
insignificant alongside the "natural desire" of Angelo and Adina.
If the story rouses any particular emotion in us, it is that of the
narrator looking back on the scandalous elopement with candid
nostalgia:

> In after years, as I grew older, I took an increasing satisfaction in
> having assisted, as they say, at this episode. As mere *action,* it seemed
> to me really superb, and in judging of human nature I often weighed
> it mentally against the perpetual spectacle of strong impulses frit-
> tered in weakness and perverted by prudence. There has been no
> prudence here, certainly, but there has been ardent, full-blown,
> positive passion. (253)

This is the most explicit statement so far of the different standards one applies to conduct in Italy, of the vacation from morality
one may enjoy there. It is not rectitude of action that is valued
in the above passage, but splendor; the narrator refuses to cen-
sure and simply relishes, without compunctions, the vitality of
"this passionate human interlude." Such an attitude is strongly
reminiscent of Stendhal and anticipates a review James wrote
only a year later, in which he remarked that the French novelist's
ruling "notion"

> was that *passion,* the power to surrender one's self sincerely and
> consistently to the feeling of the hour, was the finest thing in the
> world, and it seemed to him that he had discovered a mine of it in
> the old Italian character. . . . It is easy to perceive that this doctrine
> held itself quite irresponsible to our old moralistic canons.

According to James, Stendhal's belief that passion "combined with great energy" is "absolutely its own justification" received consummate expression in *La Chartreuse de Parme,* where we find the author's cynicism "amiable" and "enjoy serenely his clear vision of the mechanism of character" even though "every one is grossly immoral." [32]

James himself could not "serenely" accept "this doctrine" without major qualifications, but its influence on his own treatment of Italy never ceased to be profound, and is already sufficiently apparent in these five early tales. He moves steadily from uncontrolled and lavish romantic enthusiasm to a more objective and ironic consideration of his subject, simultaneously providing us with the rubrics under which all his subsequent "Italian" fiction may be grouped and understood: the voluptuous enchanting beauty of Italy and its people, the power that the past there wields over the present, the theatricalism of Italian life, the passivity and fatalism of the Italian character, its pragmatism, its talent for deception and its sexual vitality; and also the danger of idealizing Italy, of confusing Sacred and Profane Love, of attempting to emulate the Italians rather than merely observe them. For though James is delighted with the spectacle, unlike Stendhal he is not moved to participate: in "Adina" he points out Sam Scrope and clearly warns us that the celebration of moral holidays is best left to the natives.

3

The Italian Emotion
1874-1881

I

In April 1874 Henry James settled in Florence and began *Roderick Hudson* while continuing to write the travel articles later collected in *Transatlantic Sketches.* These shorter pieces are, as usual, entertaining, informative and suavely expressed, and neatly sum up his ideas on Italy to date. Buildings and statues and paintings are the predominant subject matter; James's pleasure in them is generally indefatigable, though occasionally he recoils with a shiver of romantic guilt: "There are moods," he says, "in which one feels the impulse to enter a tacit protest against too generous a patronage of pure aesthetics, in this starving and sinning world." [1]

He muses for the first time on "that Italian vice which is most trying to those who have a kindness for the Italian character—the want of personal self-respect" (218), by which he apparently means both physical and moral uncleanliness, and concludes: "If unclean manners have in truth the moral meaning I suspect in them, we must love Italy better than consistency" (257). Rome after all is filthy, yet "one loves its corruptions better than the integrities of other places" (310).

James is even further struck with the theatricalism of Italian life: everyday conversation there is "a drama, improvised, mimicked, shaped and rounded, carried bravely to its dénouement" (259), and he remarks of a nocturnal Florentine landscape that "the dimmest back-scene at the opera, when the tenor is singing his sweetest, seems hardly to belong to a more dreamily fictitious world" (273). Especially interesting is his comment on the Italian faculty "of making much of common things and converting small occasions into great pleasures"; it should be accepted by the foreigner

> as the sign of an unconscious philosophy of life, instilled by the experience of centuries—the philosophy of a people who have lived long and much, who have discovered no short cuts to happiness and no effective circumvention of effort, and so have come to regard the average lot as a ponderous fact, which may be lightened by a liberal infusion of sensuous diversion. (281–2)

Serafina, the Conte Valerio, and Angelo Beati would doubtless agree.

II

If the travel sketches indicate stasis, however, James's "first attempt at a novel" [2] takes several notable steps forward; though a deeply flawed work, *Roderick Hudson* nevertheless is of major importance in his development. It is the story of yet another American artist in Italy: young Roderick is languishing in Northampton, Massachusetts when a wealthy dilettante discerns his considerable talent for sculpture, adopts him as a protégé, and whisks him off to Rome for study. There his art flourishes astoundingly until he becomes involved with the beautiful and baffling Christina Light, who dazzles, fascinates, and finally obsesses him utterly. But Christina does not reciprocate his passion and is besides destined for a more brilliant life than he can offer. After her marriage to the Prince Casamassima Roderick loses his zest for life, rapidly degenerates both artistically and morally, and finally commits suicide by jumping off a Swiss Alp.

Reasons for the novel's failure are evident enough. The story's realism is too often disfigured by melodrama, and Roderick and his mentor Rowland so completely dichotomize its emotional range—Roderick is nearly all passion, Rowland all reason—that the reader ultimately finds both of them irritating: the disparity between Sacred and Profane Love becomes here an unbridgeable chasm. Furthermore, as F. W. Dupee remarks, "In Roderick's gigantic sculptures, his exploits in the Colosseum, his spectacular death in the Alps, James was being romantic about romanticism," a dangerous procedure observed earlier in "At Isella." [3] James himself realized the novel's weaknesses when he came to revise it for the New York Edition, whose extensively altered version is by far the superior stylistically. But basic problems are unresolved, and the question of Roderick's decline remains: why does it happen and why in Italy—what, in other words, does the setting contribute to the story?

For at first glance Roderick seems to have precisely the sort of temperament likely to profit by exposure to Italy. Rowland imagines him as "some beautiful, supple, restless, bright-eyed animal, whose motions should have no deeper warrant than the tremulous delicacy of its structure"; [4] as an artist, he intuitively possesses "the historic consciousness" (82). He is intelligent and amoral, he should succeed; but while he initially finds Italy immensely attractive and stimulating, he is finally unable to cope with it. One explanation for his breakdown is afforded by an argument with the clever sculptor Gloriani where Roderick insists that "I mean never to make anything ugly. . . . I care only for perfect beauty" (106). He reveals here a commitment to the very aesthetic idealism that ruined Theobald in "The Madonna of the Future," and it ruins both artists for the same reason: beginning as a theory, it proceeds to impose itself on every facet of their experience until it totally usurps the place of reality. In both novel and tale, the sensuous beauty of Italy tempts the hero to idealize it and then cruelly disillusions him; in the one case Italy is embodied by the slatternly Serafina, in the other by the glorious Christina Light. Roderick to be sure is scarcely as credulous as Theobald and very rightly thinks Christina supremely beautiful. What he disastrously mistakes is her nature: from her perfection of form he Platonically deduces an inward perfection that simply is not there.[5]

Thus when she jilts him for the Prince Casamassima he becomes, like Theobald, utterly apathetic; Rowland sees that "there was no will left; its place was an impotent void" (430). Furthermore, the loveliness that so misled him now tortures rather than charms, for like Sam Scrope in "Adina," Roderick finds that the only sin "this terrible Italy" punishes is the failure to be beautiful. Scrope's physical ugliness is transformed into a moral blemish by the taunt of Italian perfection, while Roderick, true to his nature, conceives his failed creativity as an aesthetic error, but the effect is the same: both feel deformed and somehow guilty in the midst of a triumphant sensuousness. This is why, when Roderick's mother seeks to distract his melancholy by remarking on the beauty of the Florentine night, he can only answer in anguish: "of course it's beautiful! Everything is beautiful; everything is insolent, defiant, atrocious with beauty. Nothing is ugly but me—me and my poor dead brain!" (416–17).

What then is the ultimate source of Roderick's failure? Rowland at one point sees him as "standing helpless in the grasp of his temperament" (200), and in the revised edition Roderick accurately terms himself a "fatalist." [6] So, in James's view, are most Italians; but Roderick's fatalism fatally lacks that precious leaven of pragmatism which keeps Italians firmly in touch with the actualities of the sensual life. For this reason Angelo Beati wins the enigmatic Adina though he loses the topaz, while Roderick Hudson loses both Christina Light and the will to create and is finally just a "nervous nineteenth-century Apollo" (195). He is James's most exhaustive portrayal of "the passion that fancies" as a terminal disease, and also the last of such portrayals; from now on the diagnosis of irresponsible romanticism will take subtler forms.

James's depiction of Italy too is heightened in *Roderick Hudson*. In his Preface, he remarks that although he began the novel in Florence, it was completed in America, and that

> as the loved Italy was the scene of my fiction—so much more loved than one has ever been able, even after fifty efforts, to say!—and as having had to leave it persisted as an inward ache, so there was a soreness in still contriving, after a fashion, to hang about it and in prolonging, from month to month, the illusion of the golden air. Little enough of that medium may the novel . . . seem to supply; yet half the actual interest lurks for me in the earnest, baffled intention of making it felt.[7]

To what extent, then, is it felt, and to what effect? Perhaps the most concentrated expression of the novel's particular Italy occurs at the beginning of Chapter IX. Rowland is musing over "the brilliant Roman winter":

> He grew passionately, unreasoningly fond of all Roman sights and sensations, and to breathe the Roman atmosphere began to seem

a needful condition of being. He could not have defined and explained the nature of his great love, nor have made up the sum of
it by the addition of his calculable pleasures. It was a large, vague,
idle, half-profitless emotion, of which perhaps the most pertinent
thing that may be said was that it enforced a sort of oppressive
reconciliation to the present, the actual, the sensuous—to life on
the terms that there offered themselves.

Yet Rowland persists in feeling

an undertone of melancholy natural enough in a mind which finds
its horizon insidiously limited to the finite, even in very picturesque
forms. . . . [He] found, in fact, a perfect response to his prevision
that to live in Rome was an education to one's senses and one's
imagination; but he sometimes wondered whether this were not a
questionable gain in case of one's not being prepared to live wholly
by one's imagination and one's senses. (155–6) [8]

Feelings of inexplicable enchantment, of sensuous immediacy,
of romantic melancholy, the temptation of passive fatalism, a
twinge of Puritan guilt—all these "American" responses can be
noted in James's earlier writings on Italy, but never before have
they been so carefully expounded and amalgamated to form a
single, coherent "Italian" emotion, which is to say, a something
one *feels* about Italy that makes no pretense of defining what Italy
actually *is*. Like James himself, Rowland has basically internalized
Italy, which he experiences as a delight but also as a threat; it
offers an "education" that questions and tests his fundamental
Anglo-Saxon values, his "passion that knows."

Italy is still, to be sure, the supreme embodiment of romance,
but romance has become almost wholly subjective, a response to
Italy rather than an aspect of it. Significantly enough, when James
revised the novel he consistently replaced the word "picturesque" with "romantic," thus making the operative agent the

viewer, not the viewed. But even in the original version of *Roderick Hudson* James never forgets how much of the Italian emotion is gratuitous, the result not of what Italy is but of what the sentimental tourist wants it to be. Rowland says of the landscape around Lake Como:

> It was all confoundingly picturesque; it was the Italy that we know from the steel-engravings in old keepsakes and annuals, from the vignettes on music-sheets and the drop-curtains at theatres; an Italy that we can never confess to ourselves—in spite of our own changes and of Italy's—that we have ceased to believe. (423–4)

This too, James now knows, may be a real Italy; it is not, however, the only real Italy.[9]

Yet if Italy is of major significance in *Roderick Hudson,* the Italians themselves are not; the novel's only true indigenes are the minor figures of Prince Casamassima and the Cavaliere Giacosa. The Prince is by far the least dashing of James's Italian noblemen: he is wealthy, ugly, and stupid, his main function being to insist on marrying Christina despite an utter incomprehension of her true nature. This weakness is skillfully exploited by the Cavaliere, an elderly, dapper, punctilious little man who dances attendance on Mrs. Light and her daughter and seems incessantly occupied with "mysterious duties." His lightly but ingeniously sketched figure manages to suggest depths of wisdom beneath a quaint, slightly ludicrous exterior, though even the revelation that he is Christina's father cannot raise his narrative status, which is distinctly of the second rank.[10] Far more noteworthy are Christina herself and the sculptor Gloriani; both these seminally important Jamesian characters reappear in his later fiction, Christina as *The Princess Casamassima* (1886), Gloriani in *The Ambassadors* (1901) and "The Velvet Glove" (1909). Their exact relation to Italy and the Italian theme is only technically problematic; clearly they are more products of an Italian environment than of anything else.[11]

Gloriani's origin is at first shrouded in equivocation. He enters the novel as "an American sculptor of French extraction, or remotely perhaps of Italian" (97), and a few pages later says of himself: "I am half Italian and half French, and, as a whole, a Yankee" (105). He is presented as a "consummately clever" and successful artist who believes that

> there is no essential difference between beauty and ugliness; that they overlap and intermingle in a quite inextricable manner; that there is no saying where one begins and the other ends . . . that it is a waste of wit to nurse metaphysical distinctions and a sadly meagre entertainment to caress imaginary lines; that the thing to aim at is the expressive and the way to reach it is by ingenuity; that for this purpose everything may serve and that a consummate work is a sort of hotch-potch of the pure and the impure, the graceful and the grotesque. Its prime duty is to amuse, to puzzle, to fascinate, to savour of a complex imagination. (98)

This aesthetic philosophy, though on a far loftier philosophic plane, strongly recalls that of Serafina's lover in "The Madonna of the Future," he of the cats and monkeys and mustachios, just as Roderick resembles Theobald in the same story. For this reason it is interesting to observe that in the original version of *Roderick Hudson* Gloriani is described as follows: "The artist might have passed for a Frenchman. He was a great talker, and a very picturesque one; he was almost bald; he had a small bright eye, a broken nose, and a moustache with waxed ends" (99).

Yet this caricature disappears without a trace in the New York Edition, where Gloriani is quite thoroughly recast in a larger mold. He is in general more dignified and less satirized, more the master-to-be than the charlatan that is, though his theories of art, it must be stressed, remain the same. The difference is that James eventually saw a new significance in "art with a worldly motive, skill unleavened by faith, the mere base maximum of cleverness" (112-13). He came to respect Gloriani's Italian pragmatism, his humane cynicism, as a valid or at least potential alternative to Roderick's impassioned romanticism. But that was in 1907; James planted seeds of greatness after the tree had blossomed. In 1874, he is quite content to tell us that "Gloriani's statues were florid and meretricious; they looked like magnified goldsmith's work" (98).[12]

Christina Light presents an even more difficult problem. It is surely misleading to describe her as "of American birth,"[13] for though her mother is American, Christina has spent all her life in Europe, and her real father, we discover in the course of the novel, is Italian. These parents seek to pressure her into a wealthy marriage, and her fitful opposition to this scheme underlies most of *Roderick Hudson's* best scenes. Christina is a woman of Cleopatra-like variety, "a struggling, questioning, *fated* female"[14] whose fate is already fixed when she enters the novel with "the step and carriage of a tired princess" (87). Her usual look is one of "imperturbable indifference"; she is considered "very clever" but also "unsafe . . . a complex, wilful, passionate creature" (169). She herself tells Rowland:

> You see I am a strange girl. To begin with I am frightfully egotistical. . . . I am tired to death of myself; I would give all I possess to get out of myself; but somehow, at the end, I find myself so vastly more interesting than nine-tenths of the people I meet. If a person wished to do me a favour I would say to him, "I beg you, with tears in my eyes, to interest me. Be strong, be positive, be imperious, if you will; only be something,—something that in looking at I can forget my detestable self." (187–8)

Yet James carefully provides us with good reasons to doubt the complete sincerity of such confessions. The worldly-wise Madame Grandoni—who reappears in *The Princess Casamassima* as Christina's confidante—suggests that "she's an actress, but she believes in her part while she's playing it" (176), and the Cavaliere, her father, tells Rowland that "she has many romantic ideas" (218). But the most important point is that "she herself was evidently the foremost dupe of her inventions" (251): Christina is victim and victimizer both, and when she encounters Rowland in Switzerland after her marriage James unmistakably invests her with the stature of one who has suffered deeply. Rowland now sees in her face

> a sinister intimation of sadness and bitterness. It was the outward mark of her sacrificed ideal. Her eyes grew cold as they looked at her husband, and when, after a moment, she turned them upon Rowland, they struck him as intensely tragical. (449)

Christina here is a genuinely tragic figure, desperately at odds with herself beneath the impassive facade of her beauty. Like Roderick she is an Italian *manqué*. Both are physically attractive, sensuously vital egotists and both are ultimately self-defeating, but for quite different reasons. Roderick is essentially weak, a genius without discipline or direction; yet while Christina says of herself, "I have no strength myself, and I can give no strength" (235), her basic flaw is hardly a lack of will, but rather its excess. Totally lacking in fatalistic serenity, her nature is powerful but mixed, committed as she is to opposing allegiances, to needs not only irreconcilable but constantly at war within her. On the one hand she craves the security and adulation that wealth and rank command, on the other she yearns to escape the restrictions and hypocrisies of a mercenary hidebound society and to pursue freely her idealistic search for "a man whom I can perfectly respect" (234).

The end result of such conflicting motives is that Christina can never seem completely sincere even to herself. Her behavior is thus a melange of theatrical flamboyance and self-deprecation, of guilt and arrogance; destructive and self-destructive both, she is a woman unable to accept fully the amoral sensuality she so naturally embodies. As she confesses to Rowland at a crucial point:

> I should like to be a princess—and I think I should be a very good one; I would play my part well. I'm fond of luxury, I am fond of a great society, I am fond of being looked at. . . . I'm corrupt, corruptible, corruption! (371)

These words recall a suggestive little tale that James wrote soon after completing *Roderick Hudson*. "Benvolio" is his only fable; its hero, a young poet, vacillates capriciously between the intellectual appeal of a girl named Scholastica and the sensual attractions of a certain Countess who is "passionately fond of pleasure and admiration": "She was clever and accomplished. . . . She represented felicity, gaiety, success; she was made to charm, to play a part, to exert a sway." [15] Benvolio is apparently James himself, once again brooding over the rival claims of Sacred and Profane Love, while the Countess is the outward aspect of Christina Light, worldly splendor incarnate, Roderick Hudson's seductive alternative to the life of art and perhaps James's too. Christina, however, seems also to express his deepest misgivings about the allure of "a great society" and evidently troubled and tantalized him as much as she did Roderick, for ten years later she will suddenly reappear in London, where her lethal beauty will continue to represent an Italy that can corrupt even those who passionately reject it.

III

After establishing residence in England James did not see Italy again until his visit in 1877, a journey that inspired the articles which later became an essay in *Portraits of Places* (1883) entitled "Italy Revisited." This piece is the finest travel sketch James ever wrote on Italy or on any other locale: the style, always suave, ranges from the evocative to the witty with utmost grace as it ponders Shelley's villa at Lerici or animadverts upon Ruskin's art criticism. The view taken of Italy, furthermore, is substantially fresh. It is true that James's first impressions are the familiar ones. "I had opened the old book again; the old charm was in the style; I was in a more delightful world," [16] he says near the beginning. Soon enough, however, he suggests that the visitor would do well to reconsider this "unspeakably interesting country":

> After thinking of Italy as historical and artistic, it will do him no great harm to think of her, for a while, as modern, an idea supposed (as a general thing correctly) to be fatally at variance with the Byronic, the Ruskinian, the artistic, poetic, aesthetic manner of considering this fascinating peninsula. He may grant—I don't say it is absolutely necessary—that modern Italy is ugly, prosaic, provokingly out of relation to the diary and the album; it is nevertheless true that, at the point things have come to, modern Italy in a manner imposes herself. (44–5)

James sees that while young Italy begins to "resent our insufferable aesthetic patronage," the old Italy "has become more and more of a museum"; and he forecasts "an Italy united and prosperous, but altogether commercial" (45). The change is already evident: "There is a horse-car from the Porta del Popolo to the Ponte Molle, and the Tuscan shrines are fed with kerosene" (48).[17] James is also more aware than ever before of the gulf between the Italy we need to believe in and the Italy that actually is. He muses that "half the time that we are admiring the brightness of the Italian smile the romantic natives may be, in reality, in a sullen frenzy of impatience and pain"; the word "romantic" here has at last taken on an unequivocally ironic meaning. The illusion is totally dispersed now, the Italian emotion completely under control, which is to say understood as completely subjective. Yet the result is not arid relativism but an increased complexity of outlook that revitalizes James's appreciation of Italy. Near Genoa, for example, he visits "a very picturesque old city upon a mountaintop" and stops to admire the view:

> There was no one within sight but a young man, who was slowly trudging upward, with his coat slung over his shoulder and his hat upon his ear, like a cavalier in an opera. Like an operatic performer, too, he was singing as he came; the spectacle, generally, was operatic, and as his vocal flourishes reached my ear I said to myself that in Italy accident was always picturesque, and that such a figure had been exactly what was wanted to set off the landscape. . . . But the point of my anecdote is that he presently proved to be a brooding young radical and communist, filled with hatred of the present Italian government, raging with discontent and crude political passion, . . . an uphappy, underfed, unemployed young man, who took a hard, grim view of everything, and was operatic only quite in spite of himself. This made it very absurd of me to have looked at him simply as a graceful ornament to the prospect, an harmonious little figure in the middle distance. "Damn the prospect, damn the middle distance!" would have been all *his* philosophy. Yet, but for the accident of my having a little talk with him, I should have made him do service, in memory, as an example of sensuous optimism! (52–3)

Slight though this episode may be, James infuses it with an admirable richness. The double vision at its heart is tersely and precisely rendered; we realize that the landscape out of which James conjures a "cavalier" does not even exist for the actual young man. The anecdote might even be fruitfully interpreted as allegory: James encounters Italy, misunderstands it, corrects his view, sees the hard realities lurking under its glamorous surface. It is true that he never put the "new Italy" to direct fictional use; imaginatively speaking, only the old Italy, eternal Italy, is of account for James.[18] But the point is that each of them sharpens his perception of the other. From now on his attitude toward Italy gradually acquires the deep hues of a photograph much exposed to light; increasingly the "sensuous optimism" evoked by the Italy of appearances is suffused with darker elements, with the sadness of increased experience and the sadness of unappeasable yearnings, with the poignance of a beauty both transient and uniquely precious, with, in short, a "sensuous pessimism."

IV

When James returned to England in December 1877, he brought with him from Rome the anecdote that was to form the basis of "Daisy Miller," which was first published the following year. This tale won its author wide acclaim as the master of the "international situation"—that is, of the fictional confrontation between old Europe and new America—and even in a way committed him to it; for the next six years James did little else except work this vein for all it could yield either financially or artistically. No wonder he called Daisy "the ultimately most prosperous child of my invention." [19]

The relationship of "Daisy Miller" to the Italian theme is curious. Its second half certainly takes place in Rome, but nowhere does the narrative give overt expression to what we recognize as the Italian emotion. The Eternal City functions mainly as a solid backdrop for Daisy's insouciant misadventures: the setting of important scenes in St. Peter's, the Palace of the Caesars, and the

Colosseum emphasizes both Daisy's total lack of the "historic consciousness," the ephemeral and thus bittersweet nature of her challenge to the world, and also the banality and pettiness of the expatriate society that so coldly snubs her. Yet the monuments themselves are not necessarily treated with reverence. When for instance the American expatriate Winterbourne visits the Colosseum by moonlight, he is at first moved

> to murmur Byron's famous lines, out of "Manfred;" but before he had finished his quotation he remembered that if nocturnal meditations in the Colosseum are recommended by the poets, they are deprecated by the doctors. The historic atmosphere was there, certainly; but the historic atmosphere, scientifically considered, was no better than a villainous miasma.[20]

The tone of this descent from poetry is pointedly ironic, especially since the "famous lines" referred to are surely from *Childe Harold's Pilgrimage* rather than "Manfred" and proceed to apostrophize Time as "The beautifier of the dead . . . the corrector where our judgments err, / The test of truth." [21] The irony is reinforced when the next instant Winterbourne hears Daisy's voice exclaim, "Well he looks at us as one of the old lions or tigers may have looked at the Christian martyrs!" (201). Daisy as it turns out is indeed a martyr, either to innocence or mere carelessness, and death does indeed "beautify" her for Winterbourne by correcting his original, coldly cautious judgment of her.

Little other use, however, is made of the Roman background, and in fact "Daisy Miller" represents a distinct change from the Italian stories preceding it. The international theme sounded so faintly by "Travelling Companions" eight years before, the conception of an expatriate American male bewildered by a lovely American girl, is here taken up again and developed into something subtle and resonant, but Italy itself plays a minor part in the result. Local color is applied sparsely, is used for contrast and not for substance; Rome provides a wry accent rather than an imposing presence. The same is true of the Italian people. Though "Daisy Miller" contains two Italian characters, Eugenio the courier and Giovanelli, they are quite ancillary to the main action; required by the plot, they in no sense help to determine it. Eugenio himself is scarcely more than a caricature of the officious, supercilious hireling who inevitably condescends if not condescended to, and his likes can be seen performing much the same minor function nearly thirty years later in *The Wings of the Dove*.[22]

Giovanelli, however, is a personage of much greater import; he is after all the lucky Italian Daisy Miller adopts as her omnipresent escort about Rome. While to her he is "the handsomest man in the world . . . tremendously clever . . . perfectly lovely!" (177), Winterbourne's first impression is rather less favorable: " 'He is not a gentleman,' said the young American; 'he is only a clever imitation of one. He is a music-master, or a penny-a-liner, or a third-rate artist. Damn his good looks!' " (181). To Winterbourne, it would seem, Giovanelli is beautiful and bogus, another Italian putting on an act; but he subsequently modifies this opinion, and tells his snobbish aunt:

> He is apparently a perfectly respectable little man. I believe he is in a small way a *cavaliere avvocato*.* But he doesn't move in what are called the first circles. I think it is really not absolutely impossible that the courier introduced him. He is evidently immensely charmed with Miss Miller. (195)

This balances our judgment but does not resolve it: Giovanelli is conflictingly viewed as both a cynical opportunist and a cap-

---

* That is, a gentleman lawyer.

tivated admirer. His final encounter with Winterbourne at Daisy's grave convinces us once for all that the question is a complex one:

> Giovanelli was very pale; on this occasion he had no flower in his button-hole; he seemed to wish to say something. At last he said, "She was the most beautiful young lady I ever saw, and the most amiable." And then he added in a moment, "And she was the most innocent." . . .
>
> Winterbourne felt sore and angry. "Why the devil," he asked, "did you take her to that fatal place?"
>
> Mr. Giovanelli's urbanity was apparently imperturbable. He looked on the ground a moment, and then he said, "For myself, I had no fear; and she wanted to go."
>
> "That was no reason!" Winterbourne declared.
>
> The subtle Roman again dropped his eyes. "If she had lived, I should have got nothing. She would never have married me, I am sure."
>
> "She would never have married you?"
>
> "For a moment I hoped so. But no, I am sure." (205–6)

Giovanelli's purpose in speaking is ostensibly to disabuse Winterbourne, and his sincerity, as far as it goes, seems complete, but as James takes care to point out, we are still dealing with the "imperturbable urbanity" of a "subtle Roman." By insisting on Daisy's innocence, he renders his own problematical; he is, in short, a puzzle, and his moral ambiguity complements on its smaller scale that of Daisy herself: she is as recklessly self-willed as he is provokingly fatalistic.

Giovanelli's is not a flamboyant characterization, but it is suggestively understated: in some ways he is made an embodiment of "that careless, irresponsible, consentingly passive element in Roman life" which James had noticed a year earlier.[23] Nevertheless it is undeniable that James purposely restricts him to a subordinate position. Giovanelli's situation is not really offered as a parallel to Daisy's but simply provides an interesting counterpoint. Americans and American concerns dominate the

Italy of "Daisy Miller"; Italians must for now be content with supporting roles.

V

Immediately after "Daisy Miller" James wrote a tale called "The Diary of a Man of Fifty" (1879), comprising the journal entries of an unnamed meditative Englishman who visits Florence after an absence of twenty-seven years and finds himself reminded on all sides of the complex amatory involvement he terminated by leaving there. This retrospective element is in itself characteristic of James's Italian mode. The first person narratives of both "The Madonna of the Future" and "Adina," for example, are introduced by a preliminary narrator who is present at a social gathering where the main story is related; what he hears in each case is a middle-aged man remembering youthful experience. James employed this rather cumbersome procedure for a specific reason: by perceptibly distancing these stories, it diminishes our sense of their immediacy and thus relaxes the stringent demands of realism. They are presumably set in the Italy of the 1840s or 50s—the Italy of Hawthorne, an Italy James never saw, never directly knew—the Italy, to be exact, of romance.

Very nearly from its origin, then, the Italian emotion is somehow associated with the sort of nostalgia felt for something that one simultaneously realizes could not quite have existed. Now, however, nostalgia for the first time takes center stage. James's diarist has been told that "I should find Italy greatly changed," but as it turns out "everything is so perfectly the same that I seem to be living my youth over again; all the forgotten impressions of that enchanting time come back to me." [24] Such an attitude is reminiscent of the essay "Italy Revisited" two years earlier, where James acknowledges the changes that have occurred there and yet feels the old fascination operate as before: in both tale and travel sketch what the narrator essentially recaptures is an Italy fabricated by predisposition rather than objectively verified.

In neither case, however, is the illusion complete. The James of 1877 is always to some extent aware of Italy's double identity and haunted by it, while in "The Diary of a Man of Fifty" an uneasy elegiac note pervades the beautifully written opening paragraph. The narrator's *recherche du temps perdu* is painful as well as pleasing: inevitably there is "a certain element of regret; a certain sense of loss lurking in the sense of gain; a tendency to wonder, rather wistfully, what *might* have been" (390). It should be evident from these words that James is here explicitly treating, for the first time, what has been called the theme of "too late," a theme that "The Beast in the Jungle" (1903) will bring to its fullest and most memorable expression.[25] Yet "The Diary of a Man of Fifty" seems to involve more than a personal lament for lost opportunities: its tone of wistful melancholy and subdued anguish suggests a valedictory tribute to romantic Italy as a whole, to the Italy that exists only in the imagination.

Here it is not even imagined directly, but is rather evoked through the memories of the narrator, who in turn is stricken with the thought that the past joy so vividly present to him was never fully realized. He is allowed to relive his experience vicariously when he meets a young Englishman who is enamoured of a beautiful Contessa, daughter to the woman, now dead, that he himself had so passionately repudiated. The Countess Scarabelli is Jamesian fiction's last native Italian for over twenty years; a spirited, enigmatic woman with "the most extraordinary resemblance to her mother" (400), she recalls the bravura of Stendhal's Duchessa Sanseverina and the moodiness of James's own Christina Light. After one meeting with her, the narrator hastens to condemn. He admits she is "altogether charming" and "the perfection of apparent spontaneity." But appearance is not reality, and the real Contessa is "an enchantress . . . an artist—an actress" (405). He asks the young Stanmer to suspect her of duplicity, he even insists Stanmer already does: "Your state of mind brings back my own so completely. . . . You admire her—you adore her, and yet, secretly, you mistrust her. You are enchanted with her . . . and yet in your private heart you are afraid of her" (408).

Clearly he is not simply imposing his own experience on Stanmer, but is also warning him against Italy in general, against the land of romantic deception and theatricalism, against the fascination of the inexplicable. The Contessa after all is a "riddle," and for a man like the narrator, inability to comprehend means inability to trust. The "ingenuous" Stanmer listens and wonders, marries the Contessa anyway, and three years later confidently asserts that it was a mistake for the narrator to have broken with the mother. It hardly matters who is correct. Whether or not mother and daughter are reprehensible, the narrator has once again made the error of applying moral absolutes to Italian situations, and must suffer accordingly.

For by now we know the reason for his rupture with the mother. He had jealously accused her of loving a certain Camerino:

> "How can he be my lover after what he has done?" she asked. "What has he done?" She hesitated a good while, then she said: "He killed my husband." "Good heavens," I cried, "and you receive him?" Do you know what she said? She said, *"Che vuole?"* (419)

Che vuole is translated by Serafina's "What will you have?" in "The Madonna of the Future." [26] It represents a vocal shrug, the voice of Italian fatalism and practicality accepting the world as it is rather than as we might want it to be. Even if the Contessa's mother reveals the lack of a "moral sense" when she subsequently marries Camerino, the narrator is nevertheless accurate in characterizing himself as a man of "too much reason." At the very end of the story his puritanical rigidity rightly preys on his conscience: *"Was* I wrong—*was* it a mistake? Was I too cautious—too suspicious—too logical? . . . God forgive me, how the questions come crowding in! If I marred her happiness, I certainly didn't make my own" (425). These Winterbourne-like doubts obviously link "The Diary of a Man of Fifty" to its immediate predecessor "Daisy Miller." Both stories depict a protagonist who overvalues "the passion that knows" to the point of becoming passionless, and both seem to demonstrate the obverse of the lesson James teaches in "At Isella" and "Adina": that moral pedantry is a grievous, even deadly sin, and that such a fault shows especially lurid, harmful and gratuitous against an Italian background. In romantic Italy, judgment is basically a destructive attitude.

VI

James began *The Portrait of a Lady* in Florence during the spring of 1880 and returned to London that June, but March 1881 found him back in Italy with a commission to write an article on Venice. This is at once the most orotund and the most exquisite of James's Italian travel pieces, for Venice, of all cities, roused him to an adoration as sensual as it is breathlessly devout. He describes his reactions to it in overwhelmingly amorous terms:

> Tenderly fond you become; there is something indefinable in those depths of personal acquaintance that gradually establish themselves. The place seems to personify itself, to become human and

sentient, and conscious of your affection. You desire to embrace it, to caress it, to possess it; and finally, a soft sense of possession grows up, and your visit becomes a perpetual love-affair.[27]

Certainly James is still aware of the "new Italy"; speaking of the restorations at St. Mark's, he speculates that "it is through innumerable lapses of taste that this deeply interesting country is groping her way to her place among the nations" (11). On the whole, however, he is given over to delight, and this time with a clear conscience. "The misery of Venice stands there for all the world to see; it is part of the spectacle—a thoroughgoing devotee of local colour might consistently say it is part of the pleasure" (3), he says, but the sight no longer prompts him to romantic guilt. He has in fact evolved a more creative, a less moralizing response to the indigence of the Italian people:

> Not their misery, doubtless, but the way they elude their misery, is what pleases the sentimental tourist, who is gratified by the sight of a beautiful race that lives by the aid of its imagination. The way to enjoy Venice is to follow the example of these people and make the most of simple pleasures. (4)

"These people," interestingly enough, absorb James's attention as never before in his travel writings. Though he still spends long hours admiring Tintoretto and Carpaccio and Bellini, he also finds time to hobnob with gondoliers, whom he finds "for the most part, excellent fellows" (19). A page later he comments on the Venetian dialect: "This language, with its soft elisions, its odd transpositions, its kindly contempt for consonants and other disagreeables, has in it something peculiarly human and accommodating." [28] "Human and accommodating"—suddenly he sees how the phrase characterizes Italy and Italians in general:

> One feels that the race is old, that it has a long and rich civilization in its blood, and that if it has not been blessed by fortune, it has at least been polished by time. It has not a genius for morality, and

indeed makes few pretensions in that direction. It scruples not to represent the false as the true, and is liable to confusion in the attribution of property. It is peculiarly susceptible to the tender sentiment, which it cultivates with a graceful disregard of the more rigid formalities. I am not sure that it is very brave, and was not struck with its being very industrious. But it has an unfailing sense of the amenities of life. (20)

This shrewdly ironic attitude is a vast distance from the priggish racism of "Travelling Companions" a decade earlier. James is not simply reconciled to the amoral humanism of Italy, he genuinely values it, and "cold-blooded stranger" though he is, "begins to lead a life that is, before all things, good-humoured" (21). This genial outlook is possible for a son of the Puritans only when he decides that Venice and the behavior of its inhabitants are best considered as theatrical rather than moral phenomena: "Then the life of its people and the strangeness of its constitution become a perpetual comedy, or, at least, a perpetual drama" (35). In his essay on Venice James sees mainly the brighter side, the comic aspect, of the Italian emotion, but he does not disavow its shadows; instead he harmonizes them with the rest of the composition. Like everything else in Italy, ethics is at bottom a matter of aesthetics.

VII

During this same Venetian visit James continued to work on *The Portrait of a Lady*,[29] which he completed later that year (1881). About half of it takes place in Italy, specifically in Florence and Rome, but the novel is not about Italy in the sense that some of his earlier work was; for one thing, all its characters are either English or American. As we have seen, James's fiction started to deemphasize native Italians in *Roderick Hudson,* and eliminated them entirely for over twenty years after "The Diary of a Man of Fifty."

There are two possible reasons for this self-imposed restriction. In the first place, it is important to remember that James's access to European society was fairly extensive in England, very limited in France, and virtually nonexistent in Italy. In a letter of 1874 he complains that his acquaintance with the Italian people is limited to "washerwomen and waiters"; this situation was ameliorated only much later in life.[30] He must therefore have relied largely on Stendhal and imaginative observation in depicting his Italian personages, and perhaps reached a point where he consciously or instinctively felt that an author with claims to the throne of Balzacian realism could no longer safely utilize such flimsy and even treacherous experience in writing fiction.

James appears to indicate as much in a review written around the time of *Roderick Hudson* which complains that Italy has "been made to supply so much . . . easy picturesqueness," and warns: "Italians have been, from Mrs. Radcliffe down, among the stock properties of romance; their associations are melodramatic. . . . We may say that the presumption is now directly against an Italian in a novel."[31] Similarly, four years later in his famous critical study of Hawthorne written soon after "Daisy Miller," James finds his predecessor's *Italian Notebooks* "of less interest than the others; for his contact with the life of the country, its people and its manners . . . was superficial." *The Marble Faun* strikes him as weak for the same reason: Hawthorne "incurs that penalty of seeming factitious and unauthoritative, which is always the result of an artist's attempt to project himself into an atmosphere in which he has not a transmitted and inherited property."[32] James may have feared that his own conception of Italy was unforgivably "stereotipato e convenzionale," as one Italian critic puts it; by 1879 in any case he had already ceased writing fictions about Italy as opposed to fictions with occasional Italian settings.[33]

Yet there may be a more positive explanation for this strange literary moratorium. In *Roderick Hudson*, where the Italian emotion finally admits its subjectivity, James's attention appropriately shifts from conflicts between Italians and Americans—as latterly in "Adina"—to the inward conflicts of Americans like Roderick and Christina Light, who show a basic temperamental affinity for the Italian ethos and yet, failing to acquire one of its requisite elements, become at once partial Italians and corrupted Americans. At the same time, the James who depicted the excesses of passionate fancy in Theobald and Roderick becomes more concerned with its lack, first in Sam Scrope, then in Winterbourne and the diarist of fifty, and finally in Gilbert Osmond. He is preparing, it seems, to portray expatriates as inured to the mixture of Italy and America in their blood, as cold and determined in their viciousness and thus trebly dangerous. Indeed, whenever we speak of Americans in James's fiction who are corrupted by Europe, we refer in every case to Americans closely connected with Italy. A character like Madame de Mauves is destructive not because she has turned French, but because she remains a rigid romantic American; Chad Newsome's selfishness at the end of *The Ambassadors* is an inherent crudity that Paris has simply been unable to refine. The actively evil Americans, however, are people like Gilbert Osmond and Madame Merle, Christina Light in *The Princess Casamassima*, the narrator of "The Aspern Papers," or Charlotte Stant—Americans pretending to Italian sophistication but lacking the innocence of a genuinely fatalistic disposition, icy sensualists who confuse Sacred and Profane Love by idealizing their own needs into absolute values. James finally decided that, to paraphrase a famous dictum of the Elizabethan era, *un Americano italianato è un diavolo incarnato:* the incarnation, however, is actually an evolution, from the self-deluded narrator of "At Isella" to Theobald to Sam Scrope to Gilbert Osmond, from untrammeled romanticism to purblind egotism.

Certainly Gilbert Osmond and Madame Merle in *The Portrait of a Lady* are superb full length studies of the genus *Americano italianato* at its most diabolic; the novel's main action turns on their deception and betrayal of Isabel Archer. Such stories are recurrent in James, and as it happens this sort of treacherous deceit always involves Italy or Italianate Americans. Besides *The Portrait of a Lady,* which is first in the series, the great Jamesian narratives of calculated deception and betrayal comprise *The Princess Casamassima,* "The Aspern Papers," *The Wings of the Dove,* and *The Golden Bowl:* all of them are either set in Italy or involve the perfidy of Italianate Americans or both. *The Ambassadors* at first seems an exception; but though Strether is indeed deceived he is not really betrayed, since Chad and Madame de Vionnet are under no deep personal obligation to him. Betrayal for James is an almost Dantean affair, the calculated falsifying of an intimate relationship by one of its partners at the expense of the other, the exploitation of the closest ties possible between human beings, those of friendship, love, and marriage, and this particular breach of faith was somehow linked in his creative mind with Italy.

The most obvious reason is that from the beginning, Italy for James suggested the inherent deceptions of romanticism. In "Travelling Companions" and "At Isella" visitors from America both need and want to be deceived, and Italians are quite willing to gratify them; in "The Madonna of the Future" Theobald the idealist is exploited by Serafina the pragmatist. In "Adina," however, the situation is reversed—the American Sam Scrope, who disavows romantic emotions as nonsense, coldly cheats the Italian Angelo Beati. From this point onward the agents as well as the victims of deceit tend to become Americans, while Italy and Italians increasingly assume the role of background.

This transferral is a concommitant of James's growing fascination with the corrupted American and perhaps of a new reluctance to depict native Italians, and it is accompanied by a sharp rise in moral pressure. Deception is excusable when practiced by Italians but execrable when the deceivers are Italianate Americans; Serafina may be forgiven even though she is perfectly aware of what she does, while Scrope must lose both his fiancée and the imperial topaz. A complex judgment supports this double standard. The Italians who deceive are openly attempting, as in the Venice essay, to make a harsh existence bearable for themselves and for us as well, and we can appreciate the bravura of their efforts. The Italianate Americans, however, are not sustained by a fatalistic acceptance of life's difficulties, but by a conscious determination to manipulate the lives of the people around them. Such Americans are Italianized in the sense that they have ostensibly adopted Italian values, but the assimilation is superficial, and what they essentially practice is the letter of the Italian ethos without its spirit. Seen in this context *The Portrait of a Lady* clearly links up with James's earlier treatments of Italy. It is significant that Isabel Archer falls prey to Gilbert Osmond for precisely the same reason that Theobald misjudges Serafina: not because Osmond is so profoundly clever but because she insists on idealizing him.

VIII

The Portrait of a Lady thus marks a thorough assimilation of Italian themes into the concerns of Jamesian fiction as a whole. There are no native characters, there is little scenic description, there is scant use of the Italian emotion; nevertheless the moral as well as physical territory surveyed is one James persistently associated with Italy. Gilbert Osmond, for instance, and to a lesser extent Madame Merle, prompt his most elaborate portrayal to date of the corruption engendered by cultural hybridization. The two strains in Osmond are American parentage and Italian upbringing; he and the Countess Gemini are the children of the "American Corinne"—a reference to the heroine of Madame de Staël's immensely popular novel (*Corinne*, 1807). The distance between the Italy of *The Portrait of a Lady* and the romantic Italy of earlier James is nowhere more measurable than in the delectable absurdity of the Countess's filial reminiscences:

> Her mother had been used to wear a Roman scarf thrown over a pair of bare shoulders and a gold laurel-wreath set upon a multitude of glossy ringlets. She spoke softly and vaguely with a kind of Southern accent; she sighed a great deal and was not at all enterprising.[34]

Her son's pretensions, however, far outstrip those of the American Corinne, and James's initial description of him finely summarizes this more subtle pomposity:

> He had a thin, delicate, sharply cut face, of which the only fault was that it looked too pointed; an appearance to which the shape of the beard contributed not a little. This beard, cut in the manner of the portraits of the sixteenth century and surmounted by a fair moustache, of which the ends had a picturesque upward flourish, gave its wearer a somewhat foreign, traditionary look and suggested that he was a gentleman who studied effect. His luminous, intelligent eye . . . would have assured you, however, that he studied it only within well-chosen limits, and that in so far as he sought it he found it. You would have been much at a loss to determine his nationality. . . . If he had English blood in his veins, it had probably received some French or Italian commixture; he was one of those persons who, in the matter of race, may, as the phrase is, pass for anything. (199)

Notable here is the *deraciné* impression Osmond immediately produces and the extent to which he appears a scrupulously created image rather than a human being.[35] The "sharply cut face" suggests the immobility of sculpture, his beard sounds determinedly Titianesque; later in the book Isabel will be struck by his "overdrawn, retouched features."

Gilbert Osmond, then, is himself the embodiment of the taste he exercises. But if James certainly believed that Italians more than any other people practiced "the art of living," just as certainly he does not believe that Osmond's life is a work of art; rather it is artificial. The Conte Valerio's monumental handsomeness, for instance, perfectly implies his stolid, amiable personality, but Osmond's carefully composed exterior hides rather than reveals. The Venetians, according to James, know how to "elude their misery," while Osmond only knows how to seem to elude his misery—beneath a facade of resignation he is rank with spite and envy. He deceives, but unlike a true Italian, he deceives himself as well as others. That particular shortcoming, indeed, taints all Italianate Americans and Italianate treachery; it stems from the application of artifice, of cold intelligence, to passionate emotions, from treating Profane Love as if it were Sacred, and from a subsequent drastic shrinking of spontaneous feeling and self-knowledge. Thus Osmond quite literally cannot see the chasm between his aesthetic ideals and ignoble actions. He can be offended by the gaudy decor of Isabel's hotel room—"the place was painfully ugly; the false colours, the sham splendour made him suffer" (268–9)—but the falsity of his own conduct regularly escapes him. Osmond's sensibilities have been dulled as much as sharpened by his lifelong cultivation of taste. The life of a "sterile dilettante" has hardly rendered him "human and accommodating"; he recurringly demonstrates a most un-Italian inflexibility. Isabel comes to realize that however she may define the ideal existence, "for Osmond it was altogether a thing of forms, a conscious, calculated attitude" (377).

Yet for all his coldness Osmond is recognizably a perversion of Italian values; he himself seems vaguely aware of the fact. Soon after meeting Isabel he outlines for her what in his opinion it means to be an expatriate:

> There were both satisfactions and drawbacks; the drawbacks were pretty numerous; strangers were too apt to see Italy in rose-colour. On the whole it was better than other countries, if one was content to lead a quiet life and take things as they came. It was dull sometimes, but there were advantages in living in the country which contained the most beauty. . . . He was inclined to think that Italy had spoiled a great many people; he was even fatuous enough to believe that he himself might have been a better man if he had spent less of his life there. It made people idle and dilettantish and second-rate; there was nothing tonic in Italian life. (217)

Whether or not Osmond is completely or at all sincere in this passage, he surely touches on the truth of his own situation. He has not, as it happens, been "content to lead a quiet life," to "take things as they came" with fatalistic resignation, and his discontent has turned him vicious. Italy has given him scope for his aesthetic interests but not for his ambitions, and over the years his indolence has become the veil of a deep frustration; he wants power and has found only beauty. No wonder he is dangerous, no wonder an Italianate American is a devil incarnate.

Osmond's pretensions are entertainingly parodied in the fatuity of his sister, the Countess Gemini. She is the other side of American corruption, its silly side; she intensifies the effect of her brother's careful, cosmopolitan suavity by constantly sounding its hollow core with her own eccentricities. She is an exaggeration to the point of absurdity of all that Osmond claims to be: he is all pose, she is affected, he is worldly, she is scandalously lascivious, he unctuously solicits the approval of the aristocracy while she hysterically implores Henrietta Stackpole to put her name in the papers. She is Osmond without taste, yet despite her shortcomings she is definitely the more attractive figure. Essentially well-meaning, the Countess can draw on a fund of humane consideration that is totally closed to her brother; if she is corrupt, she is also flexible, and to that extent has learned the lesson of Italy better than he.

Madame Merle on the other hand can be called an Italianate American mainly by courtesy of her relationship with Osmond. Her limitations closely resemble his but are less specifically derived from Italian sources. Outwardly she is a perfect simulacrum of social virtues; even so, Isabel reflects that Madame Merle "had become too flexible . . . too civilized. She was, in a word, too perfectly the social animal" (167). She is, in fact, as artificial as Osmond and has quite ceased to think of herself in human terms. "I flatter myself," she tells Isabel at Gardencourt, "that I am rather stout porcelain, but if I must tell you the truth I've been chipped and cracked!" (168). Aside from such unavoidable attrition, however, she has lost the capacity for change. When Osmond compliments her on "looking particularly well," she answers, "I think I always look the same," and he agrees: "You always *are* the same. You don't vary" (207). For all her surface splendor, Madame Merle is a completely static personality, and like Osmond she attributes her arrested development to the tenuity of expatriate existence. As she warns Isabel: "If we are not good Americans we are certainly poor Europeans; we have no natural place here. We are mere parasites, crawling over the surface; we haven't our feet in the soil" (171).

Character, then, furnishes most of the essentially Italian element in the novel, and what little evocation of the scenic or human background there is usually either supports the impression generated by the conspiracy against Isabel or else offers some sort of relief from it. A description of his Florentine villa, for instance, precedes our introduction to Osmond himself, but also anticipates it:

> The house had a front upon a little grassy, empty rural piazza which occupied a part of the hill-top; and this front, with a few windows in irregular relations and furnished with a stone bench which ran along the base of the structure and usually afforded a lounging-place to persons wearing more or less of that air of undervalued merit which in Italy, for some reason or other, always gracefully invests any one who confidently assumes a perfectly passive attitude—this antique, solid, weather-worn yet imposing front had a somewhat incommunicative character. It was the mask of the house; it was not its face. (197)

The "air of undervalued merit" is of course Osmond's own, as is the "perfectly passive attitude"; the hint of "irregular relations" and of duplicity in the word "mask" prepares us for the machinations of Osmond and his quondam mistress.

Similarly, when Isabel visits the villa she finds "something rather severe about the place; it looked somehow as if, once you were in, it would not be easy to get out" (221). Her unease foreshadows her marriage to Osmond, a marriage which in turn is figured in the outward aspect of Palazzo Roccanera, Mr. and Mrs. Osmond's Roman residence. Ned Rosier sees it as "a dungeon,"

> a kind of domestic fortress, a pile which bore a stern old Roman name, which smelt of historic deeds, of crime and craft and violence, which was mentioned in "Murray" and visited by tourists who looked disappointed and depressed, and which had frescoes by Caravaggio in the *piano nobile* and a row of mutilated statues and dusty urns in the wide, nobly-arched loggia overlooking the damp court where a fountain gushed out of a mossy niche. (319)

Palazzo Roccanera's almost Dickensian dreariness, its resemblance to a "dungeon," its "mutilated" condition, all this provides a visual equivalent of Isabel's brooding disillusionment and her sense of constriction as Osmond's wife. It is peculiarly fitting that when she contemplates the progress of her marriage during the famous fireside vigil, she should imagine Osmond as leading her "into the mansion of his own habitation":

> She could live it over again, the incredulous terror with which she had taken the measure of her dwelling. Between those four walls she had lived ever since; they were to surround her for the rest of her life. It was the house of darkness, the house of dumbness, the house of suffocation. (375)

Happily for Isabel, Italy as a whole is not transformed into a "house of suffocation" by her hideous marriage. Certainly she can never recover the ingenuous eagerness of her original response, when "Italy, as yet imperfectly seen and felt, stretched before her as a land of promise, a land in which the love of the beautiful might be comforted by endless knowledge" (195). The "land of promise" here is romantic Italy, which as we know does not really exist. As a matter of fact *The Portrait of a Lady* is unequivocally set in the "new Italy." Chapter 36, which takes up the story three years after Isabel's marriage, opens on an "afternoon, towards dusk, in the autumn of 1876." This means that Isabel's introduction to Europe and Italy exactly parallels James's first unaccompanied journey to Europe and first visit to Italy. Both the author and his creation begin their travels around 1869; both find that romantic Italy takes on a somber sheen under the pressure of close acquaintance.

How Isabel comes to feel about Italy is clearly articulated only after she has realized the failure of her marriage. Her response partially derives from that of another unhappily married and idealistic young lady, Dorothea Brooke in George Eliot's *Middlemarch* (1876), though it is in the intensity of their impressions rather than their substance that the similarity rests. For Isabel becomes very fond of Rome, while Dorothea's fervid puritanism is rudely affronted by "the gigantic broken revelations of the Imperial and Papal city": after a visit to St. Peter's she remembers, in an astonishing image, "the red drapery which was being hung for Christmas spreading itself everywhere like a disease of the retina." Eliot's heroine soon wearies of sightseeing and ends "by oftenest choosing to drive out to the Campagna where she could feel alone with the earth and sky, away from the oppressive masquerade of ages, in which her own life too seemed to become a masque with enigmatical costumes." [36] This moment may possibly have influenced a crucial scene toward the end of Isabel's history when a harrowing encounter with Madame Merle impels her to seek the consolation only Rome can offer:

> Isabel took a drive alone that afternoon; she wished to be far away, under the sky, where she could descend from her carriage and tread upon the daisies. She had long before this taken old Rome into her confidence, for in a world of ruins the ruin of her happiness seemed a less unnatural catastrophe. She rested her weariness upon things that had crumbled for centuries and yet still were upright; she dropped her secret sadness into the silence of lonely places, where its very modern quality detached itself and grew objective, so that as she sat in a sun-warmed angle on a winter's day, or stood in a mouldy church to which no one came, she could almost smile at it and think of its smallness. Small it was, in the large Roman record, and her haunting sense of the continuity of the human lot easily carried her from the less to the greater. She had become deeply, tenderly acquainted with Rome; it interfused and moderated her passion. But she had grown to think of it chiefly as the place where people had suffered. This was what came to her in the starved churches, where the marble columns, transferred from pa-

gan ruins, seemed to offer her a companionship in endurance and the musty incense to be a compound of long-unanswered prayers. (454)

This exquisite passage was transferred to the New York Edition without the least alteration, and an improvement would surely be difficult to imagine. As "old Rome" and "very modern" Isabel, view and viewer, become equal participants in a living "companionship," the Italian emotion is refined to a level of the most delicate intimacy. It no longer speaks in generalities but rather with a personal accent and warmth; it is permeated with a subtle melancholy that, while pondering its surroundings, alternately loses itself in meditation and redefines its original intensity. There is no question of delusion or wish-fulfillment—the subjective and objective elements of the experience are not contradictory but complementary: Sacred and Profane Love, knowledge and fancy, have so "interfused" that Isabel's sense of herself as a part of "the large Roman record" exactly balances the reader's sense of Rome as a part of Isabel's consciousness. The "sensuous pessimism" of her musings is triumphantly rendered; Rome is at once "the place where people had suffered" and soothingly, sustainingly beautiful. *The Portrait of a Lady,* of all James's Italian tales to date, makes the least use of local color; but perhaps paradoxically it is also the first to use the Italian emotion for purely fictional purposes, as an integral expression of character in crisis.

4

Deaths In Venice
1882-1902

I

Italy largely disappears from James's fiction for almost nineteen years following the consummate fusion of character and setting achieved in *The Portrait of a Lady*. He continued to visit there, and his love for the country remained intense, but for the time being he had little imaginative use for it. Leon Edel provides one explanation: "What was clear to him now was that the day of his little 'international' tales was virtually at an end. He could still write them but he believed he had worked that vein to exhaustion." [1] Perhaps James felt too that the Italian emotion had nothing further to yield him artistically. After 1881, in any case, the international situation, temporarily debilitated, yields the stage and withdraws into the wings of the Jamesian imagination, there to rethink old roles and con new ones, to meditate former triumphs and prepare a brilliant comeback; and Italy, duenna-like, closely accompanies both the exit and the eventual reentry.

The limbo-like state of James's present attitude toward Italy is well illustrated by two contrasting expressions it received in

1884. In February he wrote John Addington Symonds to confess that

> I nourish for the said Italy an unspeakably tender passion, and your pages always seemed to say to me that you were one of a small number of people who love it as much as I do—in addition to your knowing it immeasurably better. I wanted to recognize this (to your knowledge;) for it seemed to me that the victims of a common passion should sometimes exchange a look.[2]

This note of almost conspiratorial amorousness sufficiently testifies to an unslackened relish for things Italian; yet that summer James made his most perfunctory use of Italy in "Georgina's Reasons," a racy potboiler detailing the escapades of an unpleasant young lady from New York who secretly marries a naval officer, and, becoming gravid, runs over to Italy, bears her baby, and hastily puts him to nurse "in the Genoese hills." The father subsequently discovers that the child has been unaccountably mislaid, and spends a "year looking up and down Italy . . . and inspecting hundreds of swaddled infants."[3]

Such a plot has the virtue of rendering *Il Trovatore* nearly plausible; its melodrama echoes the common Victorian conception of Italy as the place Anglo-Saxons instinctively go to do strange, immoral, exotic things. Thus George Eliot's Gwendolen Harleth drowns her husband near Genoa, and Trollope's Louis Trevelyan goes mad on a Sienese hilltop—as Georgina herself says, "They don't mind what they do over there."[4] James makes a more sophisticated use of this particular Italy in *The Wings of the Dove,* whose two heroines are prefigured by the sisters Georgina's distraught husband encounters in Naples. Their names are Kate and Mildred Theory, and Mildred is dying of consumption.

II

Two years later, however, James briefly revived the Italian emotion in its authentic form. The protagonist of *The Princess Casamassima* (1886) is a young London bookbinder involved with anarchists and yearning after a fuller life, and the novel's crucial moment occurs when Hyacinth Robinson discovers that he is hopelessly enamoured of the old civilization he is pledged to destroy. This discovery is expressed in a letter he writes the Princess from Venice: "What an enchanted city, what ineffable impressions, what a revelation of the exquisite!" he begins, and goes on to describe lingeringly his "splendid" surroundings.[5] He assures her that "I'm very happy. . . . I don't care for anything but the present hour" (378); his revolutionary ardor has died and he can no longer pretend to uphold the "sacred cause," even though he realizes

> that want and toil and suffering are the constant lot of the immense majority of the human race. I've found them everywhere but haven't minded them. Forgive the cynical confession. What has struck me is the great achievements of which man has been capable in spite of them—the splendid accumulations of the happier few . . . they seem to me inestimably precious and beautiful . . . I feel myself capable of fighting for them. (380)

Such is the lesson of Venice for Hyacinth Robinson; at bottom it is a version, more militant in tone and more political in emphasis, of James's own "sensuous pessimism."

But the novel's primary importance for the Italian theme lies in its title character, née Christina Light, who caused the downfall of Roderick Hudson ten years before and now is brought back to perform the same function vis-à-vis Hyacinth. In his Preface to *The Princess Casamassima* James discusses her with delightful complacency and tenderness, whimsically ascribing her reappearance to "a restless vanity: Christina had felt herself, known herself, striking, in the earlier connexion, and couldn't resign herself not to strike again." [6] He obviously cherished her, and it is difficult not to share his emotion. She is as beautiful, brilliant, and intriguing as ever: Captain Sholto reintroduces us to her as "perhaps the most remarkable woman in Europe" (149), and to Hyacinth she represents the very world he so yearns for and is excluded from, its glamor, its power and its pride. She herself, however, wishes to repudiate the aristocratic milieu that has made her "corrupt, corrupting, corruption" [7] and to immerse herself in "the great social question":

> I want to learn. . . . Are we on the eve of great changes, or are we not? Is everything that is gathering force underground, in the dark, . . . is all this going to burst forth some fine morning and set the world on fire? . . . I want to know *à quoi m'en tenir.* (164)

James's Preface expatiates on this point: the Princess is inevitably "world weary, . . . and the extravagance of her attitude in these new relations would have its root and its apparent logic in her need to feel freshly about something or other—it might scarce matter what." [8] The Princess Casamassima, then, is not merely a cynical aristocrat dabbling in revolutionary politics; one must also take into account her desperate unhappiness—the Prince is as dull as he is wealthy—and her quite genuine innocence, literally her inability to discern the harm she does. For the strongest link between the two books she appears in, and the culminating tragic irony of her career, is that the woman who drove Roderick Hudson to distraction and ruin is now similarly driven: she has yielded to that fatal susceptibility of so many of

James's Italo-Americans and become a self-deluding idealist. As a result, Christina is dominated by an unconscious tendency to idealize her own basically selfish nature; she indulges her passionate fantasies in the sincere belief that she is disinterestedly seeking enlightenment. Madame Grandoni, her witty and patient confidante, calls her "an angel who came down from heaven yesterday and has been rather disappointed in her first day on earth" (203), and the analogy is astringently apt. The Princess displays the eternal freshness of a completely irresponsible person; she habitually exteriorizes all her shallowness and attributes it to the world outside, and thus can consistently view life with ever-replenished disillusion.

This is the sinister side of her "need to feel freshly." The Princess has by now perfected the simultaneous roles of victim and victimizer that she undertook in *Roderick Hudson;* she displays the same massive lack of self-knowledge, the same confusion of Sacred and Profane Love, that marks the corruption of Gilbert Osmond. Her innocence, furthermore, leaves her unable to recognize that what she really craves is excitement and power over others in conjunction with absolute freedom for herself. She wants to dominate without being dominated in return, as in her affair with Paul Muniment, and the result of this impossible desire is her eternal restlessness and self-pity: "There's nothing in life in which I've not been awfully disappointed" (217). She considers herself to have been "humiliated, outraged, tortured," and even poor smitten Hyacinth can see that "personal passion had counted for so much in the formation of her views" (220). But the fact remains that her "personal passion" is all for herself. Having idealized her own existence, she tends to treat other people as ideas too, so that when Hyacinth's belief in revolution falters, she can reject him with a clear conscience. His philosophy has failed *her,* which in her world reduces him to nullity:

"I ask him what he means by civilization. Let civilization come a
little, first, and then we'll talk about it. For the present, face to face
with those horrors, I scorn it, I deny it!" And the Princess laughed
ineffable things, she might have been some splendid syren of the
Revolution. (455)

The laughter here is almost manic, an expression of her fundamental callousness, her hard devotion to the abstract. For there
is a startling streak of brutality in the Princess. At one point she
and Hyacinth enter a pub and are confronted with "a big, hard,
red woman, the publican's wife": after they order, "Hyacinth
asked her in a low tone what disposal they should make, when
the great changes came, of such an embarassing type as that, [and
she] replied offhand, 'Oh, drown her in a barrel of beer!' " (405).

Such is the Princess's aristocracy: a moral capriciousness mas-
querading as spirited freedom, an urge to power disguised as
benevolence. But she is technically innocent to the very last,
when, seriously worried about Hyacinth, she goes seeking him
and meets the cabinetmaker Schinkel on the same errand: "The
Princess was anxious, she was in a fever; but she could still relish
the romance of standing in a species of back-slum and fraternis-
ing with a personage looking like a very tame horse whose collar
galled him." Even here the "romance" of the situation excites
her—the note of cruel condescension should not be missed either—and her further reaction to Schinkel indicates clearly the
next turn her dissatisfaction will take. "He was polite and inscrutable, quite like some of the high personages—ambassadors and
cabinet-ministers—whom she used to meet in the great world"
(591): the Princess is ready to return to her life with the Prince.

This is why Christina gives her name to the novel Hyacinth
dominates: she epitomizes the irresponsible society that drives
him to suicide. She is really as self-destructive as he, and moreover helps to cause his destruction; hence the title, and the

tragedy. Yet James does not wholly condemn her. He is becoming "human and accommodating" even about Italianate corruption, and allows us to pity the Princess as we were never allowed to pity Gilbert Osmond, even though the two of them are perhaps equally culpable in theory. Still, we must feel that Christina finally deserves the greater tenderness she inspires. We who have known her since *Roderick Hudson* realize how much of her hardness derives from an abiding sense of failure, how much of her coldness is the freezing of Italianate qualities of sensuousness, tolerance, and spontaneity under the pressure of unhappiness and frustration.

III

Upon finishing *The Princess Casamassima* James toured Italy for six months. By July 22, 1887, he was back in London, and the day after his arrival wrote Grace Norton that

> it is rather a melancholy mistake, in this uncertain life of ours, to have founded oneself on so may rigidities and rules—so many siftings and sortings. . . . Let us be flexible, dear Grace; let us be flexible! and even if we don't reach the sun we shall at least have been up in a balloon.[9]

The sentiment is candidly, joyously Italian; James himself, it appears, is becoming a pragmatist. But there was in fact every reason to be exhilarated, since he had brought with him the manuscript of "The Aspern Papers," which was begun in Florence and finished in the Venice of its setting. It is one of his most celebrated tales and perhaps the most technically perfect, fusing place and action with a thoroughness, reminiscent of *The Portrait of a Lady,* that accounts for much of its success.

As should by now be apparent, James's emotional map of Italy is largely devoted to three cities, Rome, Florence, and Venice, and of the three, Venice assumed the greatest importance as he grew older and inspired his finest fictional evocations of the Italian scene.[10] For James as for many other writers—Ruskin, Browning, Mann, Proust—Venice evokes a mood at once elusive and intense, unmistakably vivid but tantalizingly difficult to define. In Rome the literary imagination is roused by the pomp of the Church and the detritus of Imperial grandeur, in Florence by the glories of medieval and Renaissance art; but the appeal of Venice cannot be so readily ascribed to eras or institutions, unless the gondola be considered an institution. The unique physiognomy of Venice seems indeed the basis of its fascination. Again and again the literary visitor finds its watery way of life hypnotic, unreal; his most substantial impression of Venice is that Venice is the least substantial of cities.[11]

To James, it appears both Protean and strangely quiescent; the effect produced is dream-like, a suspension of the laws ordinarily governing scenic perspective and human existence and thus a visual extension of the moral holiday that Italy has always offered him. "The Aspern Papers" describes "how the sky and the sea and the rosy air and the marble of the palaces all shimmer and melt together," [12] and this hallucinatory merging is not confined to pictorial elements but also affects temporal perception. In Rome and Florence, and in Italy as a whole, the past impinges on the present, presiding over it while still remaining distinguishable from it. In Venice, however, past and present exist simultaneously rather than consecutively, overlapping and combining and changing places with the fluidity of water.

Both to the narrator of the tale and to Juliana Bordereau, for instance, Jeffery Aspern is more palpable and alive than the actual life around them. The very real loneliness and anguish of Miss Tita can scarcely compete with their obsession; as the narrator says, "I found myself falling into the error of thinking of her too as one of Jeffery Aspern's contemporaries" (319).[13] Since to James the primal appeal of Italy is romance, and since the romantic emotion is primarily a matter of self-deception, and since in Venice the deceptions of landscape induce a trance-like deceptive notion of time, small wonder that Venice for him is the most romantic and most sinister and most Italian of cities, sensuous pessimism made habitable. In "The Aspern Papers" Venice is not merely one of the story's major characters; it is the medium through which the other characters move, the thick, immobile atmosphere of sensuous decay and neurasthenic languor that deadens their responses to reality and preserves the dreams they cherish.

On the first page we hear of the Misses Bordereau living "in Venice in obscurity, on very small means, unvisited, unapproachable, in a dilapidated old palace on an out-of-the-way canal" (275), and we soon discover that the backwater they inhabit is as much a mental state as a physical location. Juliana Bordereau, venerably old, still spirited, values only the past. She tells the narrator: "I don't care who you may be—I don't want to know; it signifies very little today" (203). She feasts on the memory of her "reckless passion" for Jeffery Aspern, whom she, like the narrator, considers "a god." The coveted letters are now the sole tangible object of that passion; "She loves them," Miss Tita says, and in fact Juliana is as obsessed with them as the narrator is. Certainly in her adoration of the past she barely tolerates the present. She distinctly avers that "there is no more poetry in the world—that I know of at least" (327–8), echoing the narrator's remark that "Miss Tita was not a poet's mistress any more than I was a poet" (312–13).

The remark, as it happens, is a cruel one, since Miss Tita falls in love with the man who makes it. She alone in the story tries, however feebly, to live for the present, and she is pathetically victimized by all the idealized worship of the past that surrounds her. Living with her aunt in the "dilapidated old palace," she feels the full weight of its dreariness as Juliana and the narrator never can. "Nothing here is mine" (285), she says, and longs in her "simplicity" to escape the stifling atmosphere imposed on her: "I am not in the least fond of Venice. I should like to go far away!" (314–15). The hope she founds in the narrator, though, is inevitably frustrated. His first encounter with Miss Tita after Juliana's death takes place in the palace garden; he is "almost surprised to see her standing there in the first dusk with her hands full of flowers, smiling at me with her reddened eyes" (366)—surprised, that is, but not touched. The beautiful image does not mean to him what it means to the reader: that Miss Tita is capable of the strong, conflicting emotions which impel life forward, while the narrator feels only a single obsessive desire that leads him backward into an ever-retreating past. Her delusion, her failure, at least end in dignity and resignation; his finally lack both.

This unnamed narrator, one of James's subtlest creations, is a corrupted American who at the beginning of the story assumes the delicate task of deluding both his victims and himself. In each case he succeeds only partially, though not because of any initial scruples: "Hypocrisy, duplicity are my only chance. I am sorry for it, but for Jeffrey Aspern's sake I would do worse still" (282). Since the great romantic poet constitutes his ultimate value —"one doesn't defend one's god; one's god is in himself a defense" (277)—he is able to assure Miss Tita that his obsession with the papers "isn't for myself; there is no personal avidity in my desire. It is simply that they would be of such immense interest to the public" (335). What actually motivates him, however, is a "literary concupiscence" of which he himself is only too dimly apprised; he pursues "the responsibilities of an editor" (279) with the sort of ardor that other men reserve for sexual encounters. Beneath his courteous exterior he itches with morbid passions; at his first meeting with Juliana he thrills to the thought that "she would die next week, she would die tomorrow—then I could seize her papers" (291).

He tempers these invidious musings with complacent fantasies about Jeffery Aspern, whom he sees as "my prompter":

> it was as if his bright ghost had returned to earth to tell me that he regarded the affair as his own no less than mine. . . . It was as if he had said, "Poor dear, be easy with her; she has some natural prejudices; only give her time. . . ." My eccentric private errand became a part of the general romance and the general glory—I felt even a mystic companionship, a moral fraternity with all those who in the past had been in the service of art. (305)

This is the idiom of the young enthusiast in "At Isella," of Theobald and even of Roderick Hudson, at last reduced to its basic casuistry, and like the rhetorical flourishes of Gilbert Osmond and the Princess Casamassima it conceals a profound underlying coldness. For the end result of such smug invocations to "general romance" is that the narrator quite neglects the individual feelings of the Misses Bordereau, of whom he complains that "I had never encountered such a violent *parti pris* of seclusion; it was more than keeping quiet—it was like hunted creatures feigning death" (303). The ironic force of the simile obviously escapes him; like Gilbert Osmond, he is so anesthetized by good taste that he cannot perceive his own bad conduct. He is sincerely offended, for instance, that "with these women so associated with Aspern the pecuniary question should constantly come back" (299), but seems inclined to forgive the old woman's "coarse . . . cupidity":

Juliana's desire to make our acquaintance lucrative had been, as I
have sufficiently indicated, a false note in my image of the woman
who had inspired a great poet with immortal lines; but I recognized
after all that it behoved me to make a large allowance for her. (339)

It would be hard to say which note dominates here, the sanctimonious or the fatuous. Such insensitivity forms the bedrock of
the narrator's self-esteem; thus, while "conscious" that his servant Pasquale "had fantastic private theories about me which he
thought fine and which I, had I known them, should have thought
offensive" (354), he is not at all conscious of his own fantasies
and offensive speculations. His actions, finally, are almost as
reprehensible as his intentions; his refusal at the end of the story
to marry Miss Tita and thus gain the papers is not a triumph of
compunction but a failure of nerve. Partially because he only
visits Italy and has not been raised there, partially because his
betrayal of the Bordereau women is more contemptible than
treacherous, he is of all James's Italianate conspirators by far the
weakest, a creature so absorbed in the passions of a dead poet
that he is incompetent to deal with the passion he has aroused
in a living woman. We cannot pity the man, but we cannot hate
him either: he is too obtuse, too miserably inept.

The narrator realizes his ultimate infirmity of purpose as he
wanders stricken through Venice after Miss Tita has proposed
marriage; gazing at the statue of Bartolommeo Colleoni, he
measures himself by a former standard of ruthlessness and is
found wanting. But this incident is followed by a curious digres-
sion on local color:

I don't know why it happened that on this occasion I was more than
ever struck with that queer air of sociability, of cousinship and
family life, which makes up half the expression of Venice. Without
streets and vehicles, . . . and with its little winding ways where

people crowd together, where voices sound as in the corridors of a house, where the human step circulates as if it skirted the angles of furniture and shoes never wear out, the place has the character of an immense collective apartment. . . . And somehow the splendid common domicile, familiar, domestic and resonant, also resembles a theatre. . . . As you sit in your gondola the footways that in certain parts edge the canals assume to the eye the importance of a stage, meeting it at the same angle, and the Venetian figures, moving to and fro against the battered scenery of their little houses of comedy, strike you as members of an endless dramatic troupe. (379)

Though this passage seems at first glance an intrusion, it nevertheless serves an important function. Venice as a whole is invoked, and compared first to a private home and then to a theatre; the effect is to place "The Aspern Papers" against the huge and yet humanly accommodating perspective of an "endless" Venetian comedy, a comedy that absorbs personal unhappiness into communal "sociability." We are thus granted a glimpse of open, healthy life, of an alternative to the existence depicted elsewhere in the story. Italian theatricality is presented not only as joyous and vital, but paradoxically as real; more real at least than the closed concerns that obsess the narrator because it is the result of an impulse to share rather than to conceal, to be gregarious rather than to nurse secret fantasies. Private deceptions, James says in "The Aspern Papers," are hideous, they stunt life in the very attempt to manipulate it; and he offers as contrast the expansive public deceptiveness of Venice, which expresses life at the pitch of its everyday energy, "familiar, domestic, resonant."

IV

In the preface to "The Aspern Papers" James discusses the evolution of the tale from an anecdote concerning the old age of

Byron's mistress Claire Clairmont, and remarks on the attractions such a donnée holds for him:

> I delight in a palpable imaginable *visitable* past—in the nearer distances and clearer mysteries, the marks and signs of a world we may reach over to. . . . That, to my imagination, is the past fragrant of all, or of almost all the poetry of the thing outlived and lost and gone, and yet in which the precious element of closeness, telling so of connexions but tasting so of differences, remains appreciable.[14]

Such a past is evoked in "The Aspern Papers," but the story itself presumably takes place in the 1880s, for the narrator considers it extraordinary that Juliana has managed to "keep so quiet as that in the latter half of the nineteenth century—the age of newspapers and telegrams and photographs and interviewers" (279).

In a tale written shortly afterward, however, James once again depicts the "visitable" Italian past directly, and for the last time. "The Solution" (1889) opens with an old man reminiscing about the Italy of his twenties and a woman he loved and lost there. The situation recalls "The Diary of a Man of Fifty" (1879), but the technique is an odd throwback to the sort of framed narrative James provided for "The Madonna of the Future" (1873) and "Adina" (1874): the main storyteller is in London conversing with a preliminary narrator, a young man whom he allows to make "a note" of his "belated confession." This retrospective element, as we have already seen, is James's way of utilizing in his fiction a romantic Italy he knows only imaginatively, but now there is a distinctly morbid gleam in the backward glance. "Oh yes, you may write it down—every one's dead,"[15] says the elderly Briton in the story's opening line. This lugubrious note introduces a rather charming social comedy set "in Rome, a hundred years ago, or as nearly so as it must have been to be an episode of my extreme youth. I was just twenty-three, and attáched to our diplomatic agency there" (351). The narrator and a young French attaché decide to play a joke on Henry Wilmerding, solemn junior secretary at the American embassy. They convince him that he has compromised Veronica Goldie, an unattractive English girl, by wandering away with her during a picnic on the Campagna. The bewildered, chivalrous Wilmerding proposes marriage and is accepted, whereupon the now remorseful narrator begs his clever friend Mrs. Rushbrook, an English widow with whom he is in love, to help extricate the deluded American from a misalliance. Mrs. Rushbrook not only breaks the engagement, she marries Wilmerding herself, to the extreme discomfiture of the narrator.

As the comedy ends the morbid note returns. The narrator says of Veronica, "She is dead, poor girl, her mother is dead—I told you every one is dead. Wilmerding is dead—his wife is dead" (405). This seems excessive: if in "The Diary of a Man of Fifty" James bids farewell to old romantic Italy, we can say that ten years later in "The Solution" he methodically buries it.[16] "The Solution" represents in fact James's last fictional portrait of Rome, and is fraught with a nostalgia that threatens at times to turn as maudlin as the indiscriminate enthusiasm of "At Isella." The narrator wonders: "Is it because I was twenty-three, or because the time and the place were really better, that this period glows in my memory with all sorts of poetic, romantic lights?" He invokes "the magic of Rome . . . it is, or rather it was, the most exquisite place in the world" (351–3). Again and again a note of Arcadian enchantment suffuses the events he recalls:

> I can live over lovely evenings (oh youth, oh memory!) when tables were set for supper in the garden and lighted by the fireflies, when some of the villagers—such voices as one heard there and such natural art!—came in to sing for us, and when we all walked home in the moonlight with the ladies, singing, ourselves, along the road. (360)

The idealization here is apparent; it is also apparent that these nymphs and shepherds dance no more.

This recurring emphasis on a world and youth gone forever nearly swamps the plot of "The Solution," which at first blush seems inconsequential anyway. Actually, however, it derives from the mainstream of James's Italian preoccupations, comprising as it does a comic version of the familiar deception motif whereby a credulous hero, often American, is cunningly duped by European or Europeanized conspirators. The victim in this case is Henry Wilmerding, and the passage first describing him must give us pause:

> Wilmerding was a gentleman and he was not a fool, but he was not in the least a man of the world. I couldn't fancy in what society he had grown up. . . . If he had been turned out by one of ours he couldn't have been so innocent without being stupid or so un-worldly without being underbred. He was full of natural delicacy . . . and though he was not at all what you call a muff (he was a capital rider, and in the exaltation of his ideas of what was due to women a very knight of romance), there was something rather dove-like in his nature, suggestive of drab tints and the smell of lavender. All the Quakers . . . of whom I ever heard have been rich, and Wilmerding, happy dog, was not an exception to the rule. I think this was partly the reason why we succumbed to temptation. (357)

What emerges from this sketch, astonishingly enough, is Milly Theale in trousers: Wilmerding's idealistic innocence and "natural delicacy," his specifically "dovelike" qualities, his immense wealth and the "temptation" it poses for the Europeans around him all support the resemblance. The two characters, further-more, are the objects of similar cabals, for Milly is led to believe that Merton Densher cares for her, and Wilmerding is persuaded that he must marry the girl he has "compromised." At rare mo-ments the dialogue even reverberates with some of the complexity of James's great international tales, as when Wilmerding protests to the narrator:

> "I don't ask for the least allowance on the score of being a child of the west. I don't propose to be a barbarian anywhere."
> "You're the best fellow in the world," I continued; "but it's nevertheless true . . . that your countrypeople have, in perfect good faith, a different attitude towards women. They think certain things possible that we Europeans, cynical and corrupt, look at with a suspicious eye."
> "What things do you mean?"
> "Oh, don't you know them? You have more freedom than we."
> "Ah, never!" my companion cried, in a tone of conviction that still rings in my ears. (369–70)

There is a subtle touch in this passionate repudiation of the very ethical freedom that James sees as essentially American. Unfortunately, however, Wilmerding's character is not developed. Midway through the story he merges into the intrigue he has prompted and becomes a mere part of its mechanism, and "The Solution" ends by yielding to "something in the sophisticating Roman air which converted all life into a pleasant comedy" (369), to the seductive impetus of Italian theatricality.[17] Clearly, James was not yet ready to revive the international theme.

V

After "The Solution" begins a ten year period in James's career—1890–1900—during which he wrote nothing about Italy except a few brief travel articles and some stories, like "The Chaperon" (1891), which contain scenes set in Italy but otherwise have no importance for the Italian theme. He continued, however, to visit there often; in July 1892, for example, he wrote Charles Eliot Norton from Siena:

> I am very happy indeed to feel that—as I grow older—many things come and go, but Italy remains. I have been here many times—regularly every year or almost, for many years now, but the spell, the charm, the magic is still in the air.[18]

But there was more than "charm" for James in the Italian air during this decade: the two deepest emotional involvements of his adult life were intimately associated with Italy and the nineties. During the eighties James had met the American novelist Constance Fenimore Woolson in Florence, and lived briefly with her there under the same roof—lived alone with her if not together with her. They saw each other only intermittently after that, and in 1894, ill and unhappy, she committed suicide in Venice and was buried in Rome. James burnt all his letters to Fenimore, as he called her, and it appears he felt some responsibility for her death: it was only too possible that the frustrated and rebuffed affection of a solitary spinster had contributed to the taking of her life.[19] Five years after this death in Venice, James spent the summer in Italy and while visiting Rome was introduced to the handsome young American sculptor Hendrik Anderson, for whom the Master seems to have developed a passion none the less intense for being mostly expressed through letters. Anderson was a guest at Lamb House three times, and up until at least 1913 James persistently, yearningly invited him back. But they were seldom together, and the letters plead for the young man's presence in startlingly physical terms. "I hold you close," "I feel, my dear boy, my arms around you," "I draw you close, I hold you long"—such passages show James in a new and unique light: perhaps he was, for the first time that we know of, in love.[20]

Hendrik Anderson very possibly roused Henry James to a fresh awareness of the erotic emotion, of its imperious sway in human affairs; this awareness is certainly quite evident in his last Italian fictions, in *The Wings of the Dove* and especially *The Golden Bowl*. As for Constance Fenimore Woolson, his friendship with her and the manner of its termination doubtless colored the Italian emotion a still deeper shade of gray, emphasizing its pessimism at the expense of its sensuousness.

This darkening is understandably most evident in his treatment of Venice, which in "The Aspern Papers" is dreamy and mildly sinister but becomes far more somber in *The Wings of the Dove*. Something of this change may be glimpsed in a comparison of two essays from the nineties. The first is entitled "The Grand Canal," and appeared November 1892, about fourteen months before Fenimore's death. In it James plays the familiar "lover of Venice" for whom "Venetian life is a matter of strolling and chaffering, of gossiping and gaping." [21] To be sure he complains at the outset that "Venetian life, in the large old sense, has long since come to an end, and the essential present character of the most melancholy of cities resides simply in its being the most beautiful of tombs" (532). Immediately afterwards, however, James begins to chatter cheerfully of the Salute and Tintoretto and gondoliers, continuing fluently in this vein for some fifteen pages.

The second essay, "Two Old Houses and Three Young Women," appeared originally in *Italian Hours* (1909) though it is dated 1899, or five years after Fenimore's death. Both style and continuity are clouded, mysterious, and slightly morbid. The piece opens, for instance:

> There are times and places that come back yet again, but that, when the brooding tourist puts out his hand to them, meet it a little

> slowly, or even seem to recede a step, as if in slight fear of some
> liberty he may take. Surely they should know by this time that he
> is capable of taking none. He has his own way—he makes it all right.
> It now becomes just a part of the charming solicitation that it pre-
> sents precisely a problem—that of *giving* the particular thing as
> much as possible without at the same time giving it, as we say, away.
> There are considerations, proprieties, a necessary indirectness—he
> must use, in short, a little art.[22]

The usual "sentimental tourist" has here become "brooding,"
the image of sexual molestation is startlingly intruded, and the
reader must wonder what "proprieties" James is hinting at, what
really is there to "give away"? The faintly neurotic tone persists—the essayist of 1892 casually remarks on "the general law
that renders decadence and ruin in Venice more brilliant than
any prosperity" (548), while James in 1899 asks: "Is it the style
that has brought about the decrepitude, or the decrepitude that
has, as it were, intensified and consecrated the style? There is an
ambiguity about it all that constantly haunts and beguiles" (90).
He now prefers Venice at night and in the winter, which was
never true before: "It comes to you there with longer knowledge,
and with all deference to what flushes and glimmers, that the
night is the real time." It is especially the "real time" for riding
in a gondola:

> the movement, the darkness and the plash, the indistinguishable
> swerves and twists, all the things you don't see and all the things
> you do feel—each dim recognition and obscure arrest is a possible
> throb of your sense of being floated to your doom, even when the
> truth is simply and sociably that you are going out to tea. (91)

A few pages later James and an Englishman are strolling about
and encounter the unnamed young women, "three Sisters" with
a capital S who are "walking over to San Marco to match some
colored wool" (97). James has met them before; they are impoverished Venetian nobility and invite him and his friend to "their

sequestered home," pointing out on the way a house where George Sand once lived with Alfred de Musset. James is naturally intrigued, and yet wonders

> why we have so continued to concern ourselves, and why the fond observer of the footprints of genius is likely so to continue, with a body of discussion, neither in itself and in its day, nor in its preserved and attested records, at all positively edifying. (99)

Is James glancing obliquely, even unconsciously, at his relationship with Constance Fenimore Woolson? The whole essay remains suggestive and perhaps symbolic, dream-like and disjunct, vaguely intense and utterly opaque. Like so much of James's late travel writing it gives the effect of fiction rather than of travelogue; despite the claims of the opening paragraph it savors more of nerves than of art. Yet its meaning is perhaps ultimately decipherable in *The Wings of the Dove,* whose Venice is also mysterious, fateful and threatening.

VI

In 1899, during the summer of his meeting with Hendrik Anderson, James called on Mrs. Humphry Ward at her villa near Rome and inspired his hostess to rhapsody:

> here is this Italian country, and in the Eternal City, the man whom I had so far mainly known as a Londoner was far more at home than I. . . . Roman history and antiquities, Italian Art, Renaissance sculpture, the personalities and events of the Risorgimento, all these solid *connaissances* and many more were to be recognized perpetually as rich elements in the general wealth of Mr. James's mind.[23]

This formidable *cognoscente* was, as it happened, currently examining the memorabilia of William Wetmore Story, the deceased

American sculptor, whose biography he had already undertaken to write.[24] He eventually did so in 1903; but the Story relics had perhaps a more immediate effect on him. At any rate sometime around 1900 James quite suddenly revived the international theme nearly two decades after he had effectively laid it to rest with *The Portrait of a Lady*. What might be regarded as an earlier revival—that represented most notably by "The Aspern Papers" —was instigated during a visit to Italy in 1887, and it may be more than coincidental that upon his return from the Italian sojourn of 1899 James began to mull over seriously the donnée of *The Ambassadors*, which had been entered in his Notebooks as early as October 1895.

First, however, he rummaged even further back in the Notebooks to February 1895 and wrote a sort of warm-up exercise. "Miss Gunton of Poughkeepsie" (1900) is barely fifteen pages long; yet like "The Solution" it demonstrably serves as a miniature prologue to the swelling act of the Major Phase. The story is simple to the point of inconsequence: Lily Gunton, a "charming American girl" [25] of immense wealth, is pursued across Europe by an ardent Italian prince whose offer of marriage she finally accepts in London. He then asks her to write his mother, an inflexibly proud Roman matriarch, but Miss Gunton insists that it is his mother's place to write first and welcome a stranger into the family. Both women stand firm, and on this pebble of contention the engagement founders; Miss Gunton returns to America and the Prince is left disconsolate.

James fleshes out this bare anecdote with swift sharp characterization. Lily Gunton is a heroine who is "afraid I want a good many things" but is not at all afraid to go after them; she impresses her friend Lady Champer as "amazingly free" and yet "incalculable":

Old measures and familiar rules were of no use at all with her—she had so broken the moulds and so mixed the marks. What was confounding was her disparities—the juxtaposition in her of beautiful sun-flushed heights and deep dark holes. (78–9)

Miss Gunton in short is Daisy Miller with a high polish, a new degree of hardness. She says of the Prince, "Unless he wants me more than anything else in the world I don't want him" (79), and this proviso necessarily entails the indulgence of her whims at the expense of his mother's. When Lily stubbornly refuses to write, Lady Champer chides her lack of the "historic sense":

> I think you ought to remember that you're entering a very great house, of tremendous antiquity . . . the heads of which . . . are accustomed to a great deal of deference. The old Princess, my dear . . . is a most prodigious personage.

Miss Gunton's answer is puzzling: "Why Lady Champer, of course she is, and that's just what I like her for!" (85). At the end of the story her ladyship tells the Prince she believes the puzzle can be resolved. Lily never loved the Prince; what attracted her was "your great historic position, the glamour of your name and your past. Otherwise what she stood out for wouldn't be excusable. But she has the sense of such things, and *they* were what she loved." And yet she obviously did not love them enough. In the face of such contradictions the only possible response is that expressed in the story's last line: "With Americans one is lost!" (92).

The Prince, who is the first native Italian in James's fiction since "The Diary of a Man of Fifty" (1879), is perhaps even more interesting than his fiancée and certainly more comprehensible:

> Tall, fair, active, educated, amiable, simple, carrying so naturally his great name and pronouncing so kindly Lily's small one, the happy

youth, if he was one of the most ancient of princes, was one of the most modern of Romans. (81)

Yet the Prince's modernity ultimately falls victim to his strong "family sense"; Lady Champer touches him on a sore point when she inquires: "My dear young man, are you afraid of your mamma?" (88). The Prince is in truth "devoted to his mother, *a l'italienne,*"[26] as James remarks in his Notebooks, though he also loves Lily. Acknowledging the claims of both Italy and America, tradition and the future, he finds himself a soft and ineffectual mediator between two implacable women.

For the first time in Jamesian fiction, then, Italy is actually at the mercy of America, which leads Lady Champer to suggest that the Prince had better abandon the pursuit of American women:

> "They're an interest. But they're a nuisance. It's a question, very certainly, if they're worth the trouble they give."
>
> This at least he could take in. "You mean that one should be quite sure first what they *are* worth?"
>
> He made her laugh now. "It would appear that you never *can* be. But also really that you can't keep your hands off."
>
> He fixed the social scene an instant with his heavy eye. "Yes. Doesn't it?"
>
> "However," she pursued as if he again a little irritated her, "Lily's position is quite simple."
>
> "Quite. She just loves me."
>
> "I mean simple for herself. She really makes no differences. It's only we—you and I—who make them all."
>
> "But she tells me she delights in us; has, that is, such a sense of what we are supposed to 'represent.' "
>
> "Oh, she *thinks* she has. Americans think they have all sorts of things; but they haven't. That's just *it*"—Lady Champer was philosophic. "Nothing but their Americanism. If you marry anything you marry that." (89)

In this significant conversation even more than in its plot, "Miss Gunton of Poughkeepsie" figures as a comic prelude to *The*

Golden Bowl, where another "modern" Roman prince is involved with yet another wealthy American girl. Her "worth" too is problematical: after they marry and settle in London he is amazed at how being his wife "makes no differences" in the way she lives. James's little tale of 1900 only sketches the enigma that "Americanism" poses for the Italian mind; it is a theme that his last major novel will develop at length.

VII

In his original notation of the donnée for *The Ambassadors* (October 31, 1895), James muses: "I don't altogether like the *banal* side of the revelation of Paris—it's so obvious, so usual to make Paris the vision that opens the hero's eyes, makes him feel his mistake. It might be London—it might be Italy." But a little later he yields the point—"I'm afraid it must be Paris, if he's an American." [27] Italy, he may have felt at this point, would prove too equivocal or even sinister a setting: Strether's impression must be of a place where the life he has missed is lived, and not, as in Isabel Archer's Rome, of a place where people have suffered.

Italy does, however, make one contribution to the plenitude of experience with which Paris overwhelms Lambert Strether, for it is during a Sunday afternoon reception in Gloriani's garden that he is moved to urge Little Bilham, in the novel's central passage, "Live all you can; it's a mistake not to." [28] Gloriani is the ingenious sculptor of *Roderick Hudson* (1875) almost thirty years later; like Christina Light in the same book he apparently refused to remain a "spent puppet." [29] While the earlier novel hedges on his national origin, in *The Ambassadors* he becomes unqualifiedly Italian: we are told that "after an earlier time in his native Rome he had migrated, in mid-career, to Paris" (196).

Formerly too, he was something of a mountebank; now by contrast he is "the great Gloriani . . . the celebrated sculptor" (193), a man and artist of unquestioned eminence, distinction and magnetism. The reason for these adjustments is obviously that James now respects him, and not least for exemplifying certain essentially Italian qualities.

Furthermore, Strether's impressions of his host in a sense recapitulate James's own gradual penetration of Gloriani's significance. There is, to begin with, the "fine worn handsome face," which affects the American "as a dazzling prodigy of type"—the type, that is, of the famous man, the public personage who shines "with the light, the romance, of glory" (196). An instant later, though, Strether is "held by the sculptor's eyes" and subjected to "the deepest intellectual sounding to which he had ever been exposed. . . . The deep human expertness in Gloriani's charming smile—oh the terrible life behind it!—was flashed upon him as a test of his stuff" (197). The challenge Gloriani offers is that of complete coherence; his artistic sensibility and "human expertness" are indistinguishable components of a single mind. The "life" perceived in his smile is "terrible" because like Matthew Arnold's Sophocles he has seen it steadily and seen it whole. He has never falsified it with theories as his former colleague Roderick Hudson did, never been tempted to "nurse metaphysical distinctions" or "caress imaginary lines"; in T. S. Eliot's phrase, he has "a mind so fine that no idea could violate it." [30] A triumphant product of Italian pragmatism, of a "human and accommodating" sensuous pessimism, he displays a total fusion of Sacred and Profane Love, of experience and imagination, and perhaps ultimately represents the sort of artist James himself aspired to be.

Did James also aspire to Gloriani's other preeminent qualities? Soon after Strether's introduction to the sculptor, Little Bilham remarks on the "awfully nice women . . . the right *femmes du monde*" that Gloriani attracts to his receptions: "You can fancy his history on that side—I believe it's fabulous: they *never* give him up" (199). Later on Strether glimpses "the great artist" in conversation with a Duchess, and senses something "covertly tigerish, which came to him across the lawn and in the charming air as a waft from a jungle. Yet it made him admire most of the two, made him envy, the glossy male tiger, magnificently marked" (219). The indication here of Gloriani's sexual prowess is unmistakable. The image of the tiger renders his sensuality both beautiful and ruthless, another one of those inevitabilities he deals with so gracefully and so unflinchingly. Gloriani figures directly in *The Ambassadors* for something less than two pages and never even speaks, but for Strether and the reader alike he leaves an uneffaceable impression of amoral energy and aesthetic vitality.

James uses Gloriani yet again in one of his last tales, "The Velvet Glove" (1909), where he appears only peripherally and is little more than a vague venerable presence, "the great Gloriani," [31] who entertains in his Parisian studio on a lavish scale. At one of his fetes the rising young American novelist John Berridge is dazzled by the attentions of a beautiful Princess who, far from being the "Olympian" he supposes, is the conniving authoress of a romance entitled *The Velvet Glove;* all she wants from him, it turns out, is a "lovely, friendly, irresistible log-rolling Preface" (259) for her book. The humiliated Berridge refuses, and tells her: "You *are* Romance. . . . Don't attempt such base things. Leave those to us. Only live. Only be. *We'll* do the rest" (263). He then kisses her passionately and rushes away. For those who remember the Princess that Roderick Hudson and Hyacinth Robinson so disastrously idealized, the linking of Gloriani with the collapse of Berridge's "romantic structure" (240) is both ironic and appropriate.

VIII

The Wings of the Dove (1902) is James's last work of fiction to utilize Italy as a setting: about a quarter of the action unfolds in a romantically sinister Venice that is unique among his portraits of places. Once again the heroine is a spirited and fabulously rich American girl who survives the blandishments of English society, refuses a lord, and then, transplanted to Italy, becomes the victim of a conspiracy that has been hatched by a man and woman secretly in league with each other. To this extent the story is a rewriting of *The Portrait of a Lady,* though the details of the paradigm differ. The dove-like Milly Theale is fatally ill, and thus absorbs the special pathos that attaches to Ralph Touchett in the earlier novel; yet her deceivers, Merton Densher and Kate Croy, are considerably less despicable than Gilbert Osmond and Madame Merle.

James's conception of Italianate treachery obviously underwent a marked development between 1881 and 1902. A clear sign of this obtains at the very beginning of the Venetian episode in *The Wings of the Dove* when we encounter Milly's major-domo Eugenio. Like Gloriani he is an Italian character revived from an earlier work and endowed with greater dignity and significance. In 1878 he appeared briefly as courier to the Miller family in "Daisy Miller"; "a tall, handsome man, with superb whiskers," he was lofty with Winterbourne and condescending to his employers.[32] Twenty-four years later James spectacularly refurbishes him into "the great Eugenio, recommended by granddukes and Americans"; still arrogant, he is now a genuinely formidable figure, "polyglot and universal, very dear and very deep." [33] Milly herself feels greatly indebted to him, despite his air of "a swindler finished to the fingertips,"

for he was for ever carrying one well-kept Italian hand to his heart
and plunging the other straight into her pocket, which, as she had
instantly observed him to recognise, fitted it like a glove. . . .
Gracefully, respectfully, consummately enough—always with hands
in position and the look, in his thick neat white hair, smooth fat face
and black professional, almost theatrical eyes, as of some famous
tenor grown too old to make love, but with an art still to make
money—did he on occasion convey to her that she was, of all the
clients of his glorious career, the one in whom his interest was most
personal and paternal. The others had come in the way of business,
but for her his sentiment was special. Confidence rested thus on her
completely believing that: there was nothing of which she felt more
sure. (133–4)

The wit and delicacy of this character sketch are placed at the
service of the novel as a whole. James intends us to feel Eugenio's
complexity: he is a "swindler" who gives value for money, he is
completely mercenary and yet staunchly loyal to Milly. The "theatrical" aura he exudes is typically Italian in that it seems an
effect, not of falsity, but of flamboyance, of self-dramatization;
he does not after all bother to conceal his venality, but rather
revels openly in the skill with which he exercises it. He delights
himself and delights Milly too, and James gives us every reason
to believe that "for her his sentiment was special." The point is
that Eugenio is simultaneously motivated by "the general tact of
a residuary legatee" and by an intensely "personal and paternal"
devotion to Milly; the inextricable combination of these two elements renders him "abysmal" but not insincere. If he exploits
his employer he at least does so frankly and openly, with her full
knowledge and even approval, while her British friends cover
their exploitation with elaborate cosmetic rationalizations. Milly
at one point feels Eugenio urging her to "some complete use of
her wealth . . . . It had passed between them as preposterous
that with so much money she should just stupidly and awkwardly

want—any more want a life, a career, a consciousness, than want a house, a carriage or a cook" (142). Such absolute materialism may be crude, but it is uncomfortably close to the actual though dissimulated beliefs of Densher and of Kate especially.

Densher himself finds he must endure the withering contempt of Milly's "most devoted servant" when he is refused admittance to her, though what especially galls him is not so much the snub as "the fact that one very acute person in the world, whom he couldn't dispose of as an interested scoundrel, enjoyed an opinion of him that there was no attacking, no disproving, no—what was worst of all—even noticing" (260). Thereafter he dreads having to face the major-domo's "maintained observation": this "very acute person" has by then become an embodied rebuke of British duplicity and a superlative example of the major function a minor character can perform in James. For Eugenio sets a standard against which the other people around Milly can be measured and found wanting; ironically enough, he is the only one of the entourage who is completely honest with her. Like Italy itself his morality is human and accommodating, like Italy too he is the victimizer and enchanter of tourists, he is deception incarnate, which means deception so obvious and wholesale that it fools only those who want to be fooled. Compared to Densher and Kate, Eugenio is harmless; his bad motives hurt Milly far less than their good intentions.

Eugenio rightly desires to protect his vulnerable mistress from others; what he cannot know is that she needs protection from herself as well. Frederick C. Crews calls Milly Theale "the most romantic and ethereal heroine in all Jamesian fiction," [34] and the designation is appropriate in two senses: Milly's complex fate is viewed romantically by those around her and also provokes her own imaginative reveries. It is thus nearly inevitable that she should end her life in Venice, the most romantic city of the most romantic country on earth. But it must be stressed that nowhere else in his fiction is James more emphatic about the dangerous deceptiveness of romance. On the one hand he shows us how Milly's romantic appeal evidently allows people to admire and even use her as if she were some merely aesthetic phenomenon, to enjoy her like a painting or opera; on the other, he intimates that Milly's own sense of her romantic predicament is morbidly opposed to a healthy involvement with reality. Thus in the first two chapters of the Venetian episode we see her "systematic bravado" subjected to the temptation of Italian beauty as she moves through Palazzo Leporelli "slowly to and fro as the priestess of the worship" (135):

> It all rolled afresh over Milly: "Oh, the impossible romance—!" The romance for her, yet once more, would be to sit there for ever, through all her time, as in a fortress; and the idea became an image of never going down, of remaining aloft in the divine, dustless air, where she would hear but the plash of water against stone. (147)

At times, however, the "romance" seems possible enough: "I think I should like," says Milly, "to die here" (151). We have reached the opposite extreme of "At Isella," where yielding to romance was viewed in some sense as an affirmation of life; by now the romantic emotion has developed into a yearning for ultimate aesthetic stasis and has become a sort of death-wish.

Of course we pity Milly, and understand why she is so tempted to abandon "the passion that knows" for a complete immersion in the fancies that Palazzo Leporelli stimulate. But our pity should not prevent us from recognizing that Densher's subsequent deception of her skillfully exploits her own self-deception, her need to be deceived. At a late point in the conspiracy he is even impressed by how "Milly herself did everything":

> Something indeed incalculable wrought for them—for him and Kate; something . . . ever so much better than they: which wasn't a reason, however—its being so much better—for them not to profit by it. Not to profit by it would . . . have been to go directly against it; and the spirit of generosity at present engendered in Densher could have felt no greater pang than by his having to go directly against Milly. (239)

In this passage Densher manages to give the best of reasons for perpetrating the worst of betrayals; the whole plot against Milly, in fact, is a triumph of such utilitarian romanticism, which is to say a monstrous confusion of Sacred and Profane Love. Everyone involved knows the basic situation—that Milly is going to die, that Densher could console her if he would, that he and Kate are intimate—and everyone resolutely swathes their knowledge in glittering fantasies that make reality more attractive but also more elusive, more difficult to deal with when it finally becomes imperative to do so. Italianate treachery, it would seem, has extended its net to include victimizers as well as victims: though Gilbert Osmond and Madame Merle were outside the plot they spun and cold-bloodedly resolved on Isabel's deception, Christina Light and the narrator of "The Aspern Papers" are progressively entangled with the delusions they seek to foster, and in *The Wings of the Dove* betrayers and betrayed struggle side by side with intrigues that ultimately confound them all. This is the "evil of the normal" that J. A. Ward talks about: [35] Milly deceives herself and Susan Stringham anxiously assists, Kate nobly confesses that "I don't like it, but I'm a person, thank goodness, who can do what I don't like," whereupon Densher thinks her "heroic" (226).

It is this sort of sophistry that leaves him impervious to Milly's true needs until in his last conversation with her he is suddenly aware of "the drop, almost with violence, of everything but a sense of her own reality" (247). Reality at this point can only be a revelation; Densher now comprehends, too late, how hideously Milly has been used:

> He had not only never been near the facts of her condition . . . but he had also, with everyone else, as he now felt, actively fostered suppressions which were in the direct best interest of everyone's good manner, everyone's pity, everyone's really quite generous ideal. (298–9)

He sees at last that the "ideal" has all along been a euphemism, that tasteful exploitation, compassionate deception, are exploitation and deception all the same; for the first time he gazes beyond the veil of polite fanciful pretense at "the facts of physical suffering, of incurable pain" (299). For both Milly and himself romantic illusion is ended, and in its place is the special bitterness of truth too long deferred.

The taste of it belongs above all to Densher: his point of view is assumed in the last three books of the novel and thus dominates the Venetian episode. Throughout it he is largely distracted from consideration for Milly by the crisis of his relations with Kate, whose "management" of him inspires a "rebellion" that ends in "conquest": Kate yields to an ultimatum and they make love together once before she and Aunt Maud return to London. The consummation of Densher's lust is one of those indiscretions, unthinkable at home, that Anglo-Saxons find it easier to commit in Italy, and it marks James's first extended treatment of sex in his fiction. Even so, the tryst is not presented directly but by implication, through Densher's haunted consciousness of it: "What had come to pass within his walls lingered there as an obsession importunate to all his senses; it lived again, as a cluster of pleasant memories, at every hour and in every object; it made everything but itself irrelevant and tasteless" (235). The evocation of this "obsession" is remarkably vivid and suggestive:

> The door had but to open for him to be with it again and for it to be all there; so intensely there that, as we say, no other act was possible to him than the renewed act, almost the hallucination, of intimacy. Wherever he looked or sat or stood . . . it was in view as, when the curtain has risen, the play on stage is in view, night after night, for the fiddlers. He remained thus, in his own theatre, in his single person, perpetual orchestra to the ordered drama, the confirmed "run"; playing low and slow, moreover, in the regular way, for the situations of most importance. (236–7)

There is no direct mention here of Italy's association with the sensual and theatrical or of the hallucinatory effect of Venice, for they have imperceptibly merged into the specific derangement of a specific mind: the quality of dream-like eroticism in "the renewed act" seems an intensification of the Italian emotion itself.[36]

It is questionable, indeed, whether there is any "real" Italian landscape in the novel at all, as there is in *The Portrait of a Lady* and even in "The Aspern Papers," since Densher's interior Venice, the Venice of his deluded morality and erotic obsessions, is counterparted by a supposedly exterior Venice that yet mirrors his every shift of feeling with strange exactitude. His exuberant challenge to Kate's "management," for instance, takes place "in the middle of Piazza San Marco, always, as a great social saloon, a smooth-floored, blue-roofed chamber of amenity, favourable to talk" (189). This is "the splendid Square, which had so notoriously, in all the years, witnessed more of the joy of life than any equal area in Europe" (193), an idea echoed by the introduction James wrote to an article on "Browning in Venice" published in February 1902:

It is a fact that almost everyone interesting, appealing, melancholy, memorable, odd, seems at one time or another, after many days and much life, to have gravitated to Venice by a happy instinct, settling in it and treating it, cherishing it, as a sort of repository of consolations. . . . The deposed, the defeated, the disenchanted, the wounded, or even only the bored, have seemed to find there something that no other place could give.[37]

Thus James the casual essayist. A decade later in *The Wings of the Dove*, he dramatizes this conception of Venice as a "repository" of unhappy experience by linking it with Densher's miserable ramble through the Piazza after he is denied admittance to Palazzo Leporelli:

There were stretches of the gallery paved with squares of red marble, greasy now with the salt spray; and the whole place, in its huge elegance, the grace of its conception and the beauty of its detail, was more than ever like a great drawing-room, the drawing-room of Europe, profaned and bewildered by some reverse of fortune. (261)

Subjective intensity and precise objective detail here become confounded and inextricable, a process that began as Densher was first turned away from Milly's door and felt, in the "cold, lashing rain," a "Venice all of evil" (260).

Given this peculiar intensity the effect is all the more powerful when, several days after Milly's collapse, the weather changes:

the stubborn storm yielded, and the autumn sunshine, baffled for many days, but now hot and almost vindictive, came into its own again and, with an almost audible paean, a suffusion of bright sound that was one with the bright colour, took large possession. (294)

We realize here, in the startling force of words like "baffled" and "vindictive," that this Venice is actually Densher's long-suppressed conscience mocking him with a cruel juxtaposition of the renewed "sunshine" and Milly's agony, just as the "Venice all of evil" was in essence Densher's evil at large in a suggestive environment. What this finally means is that unlike the Italian settings in James's other fiction, the Venice of *The Wings of the Dove* is basically hallucinatory. Instead of the serenity, the noble and yet human scale of Rome in *The Portrait of a Lady,* we find hysterical extremes of glitter and gloom; people do not interact with landscape so much as they are overwhelmed by it, exhilarated one minute, chastised and derided by it the next. Knowledge and fancy are not fused but rather jumble together, making the exterior world behave as if it were a mere projection of human hope, guilt, lust, and fear. Isabel Archer and Rome enter into a gentle "companionship," but Densher's acquaintance with Venice is tense, even hostile, and strangely phantasmagoric.

James's fictional farewell to Italy, then, is somber and memorably vivid, and clearly a further step in that tendency of the Major Phase to internalize scenery as well as action. It is also his harshest indictment of the romantic viewpoint as a gloss for betrayal; yet at the same time we are meant to admire Densher's romantic idealization of the dead Milly, as indeed we do. James still seems to need it both ways, and it is only in *The Golden Bowl* that he will at last find a stable balance between romance and reality. *The Wings of the Dove* does, however, make one definitive discrimination: it investigates with supreme authority the complex deceptions and self-deceptions of the Italianate treachery which is yet not a part of Italy itself. We glimpse the real Italy in the candidly conniving Eugenio, and once in the face of Milly's handsome gondolier, Pasquale, who greets Densher on the day she refuses to see him with an expression that would be blank "if the term could ever apply to members of a race in whom vacancy was but a nest of darknesses—not a vain surface, but a place of withdrawal in which something obscure, something always ominous, indistinguishably lived" (256). This comment is a promise; in James's next and last great novel, the "nest of darknesses" will be illuminated and the "something always ominous" will at last emerge from its "place of withdrawal" into the open.

5

A Congruous Whole
1903-1909

I

In 1901, while working on *The Ambassadors,* James published a short travel sketch entitled "The Saint's Afternoon." Now consistently referring to himself as "the brooding tourist," [1] he here records his 1899 visit to "beautiful, horrible, haunted" Capri (483), an experience which seems "like some supreme reward of an old dream of Italy" (485). The tone is both serene and slightly melancholy. James again notes the ubiquitous theatricalism as St. Anthony's image is borne in procession from the local church: "we waited as densely for him to come out, or rather to come 'on,' as the pit at the opera waits for the great tenor" (488). He is struck anew by "that special civilized note—the note of manners—which is so constantly touched" (490); most importantly, he feels "afresh the old story of the deep interfusion of the present with the past," a feeling which became more and more frequent with him from this point on.[2] Yet in the midst of an exhilarating *festa* he is moved to wonder whether "abysmal old Italy" is really abysmal after all:

The beauty and the poetry, at all events, were clear enough, and the extraordinary uplifted distinction; but where, in all this, it may be asked, was the element of "horror" that I have spoken of as sensible?—what obsession that was not charming could find a place in that splendid light, out of which the long summer squeezes every secret and shadow? I'm afraid I'm driven to plead that these evils were exactly in one's imagination, a predestined victim always of the cruel, the fatal historic sense. (493)

He might more accurately have said a victim of romanticism, for James it seems is still deeply troubled by his passionate fancies about Italy.

About this time James also wrote his only critiques of Italian literature, a long essay on Gabriele d'Annunzio and a shorter one on Matilde Serao. He finds much to admire in these novelists, particularly their zest and bravura, yet both finally constitute for him a "case" that is also a warning.[3] James does not object to their frank treatment of *"passione"* (303), of "acutely sexual" (271) human relations; what bothers him is their tendency to depict what he calls in a wondrous phrase "mere zoological sociability" (287): "The effect then, we discover, of the undertaking to give *passione* its whole place is that by the operation of a singular law no place speedily appears to be left for anything else" (309). The longer essay as a matter of fact contains James's most explicit and extended pronouncement on the place of sex in fiction. He complains of d'Annunzio:

That sexual passion from which he extracts such admirable detached pictures insists on remaining for him *only* the act of a moment, beginning and ending in itself and disowning any representative character. From the moment it depends on itself alone for its beauty it endangers extremely its distinction, so precarious at the best. For what it represents, precisely, is it poetically interesting; it finds its extenuation and consummation only in the rest of life. Shut out from the rest of life, shut out from all fruition and assimilation, it has no more dignity than—to use a homely image—the boots

and shoes that we see, in the corridors of promiscuous hotels, standing, often in double pairs, at the doors of rooms. (292)

We are reminded of Max Beerbohm's famous cartoon of Henry
James earnestly pondering two pairs of shoes left outside a closed
bedroom door, and also of how at this period he wove Merton
Densher's erotic obsession into the larger fabric of *The Wings of
the Dove*.[4] But James most memorably relates "sexual passion"
to "the rest of life" in the novel about an Italian prince and
princess he is soon to begin.

II

On January 6, 1903 James wrote Mrs. Waldo Story, daughter-in-
law of the late William Wetmore Story, that he had "got on so
straight with the Book that three quarters of it are practically
written, and four or five weeks more will see me, I calculate, at
the end of the matter." [5] The "Book" is *William Wetmore Story and
His Friends,* which after numerous delays he finally settled down
to write before starting *The Golden Bowl*.[6] He chose this particular
moment to fulfill an obligation contracted in 1897 partially because the moment was at last ripe: "The thing has been made
possible by the lapse of time," he told Mrs. Story,[7] and as it
happens *William Wetmore Story* logically occupies a central position
in the revaluation of the international situation, and of the Italian
experience, represented by the three long novels of the Major
Phase. *The Ambassadors* is its precursor to the extent that both
present a Europe populated by ghosts: Strether's Paris is made
vivid by memories of his first visit abroad and regrets for what
might have been, while Story's Rome is part of a past that has
saddened the present by its disappearance—it is the Rome of
"The Solution," "sweeter, softer, easier, idler," [8] "the old Rome

of the old order" which shows "a face inexpressibly romantic"
(I. 93). And *William Wetmore Story* is clearly linked to *The Wings
of the Dove* in its sense of Italy's equivocal nature as a spiritual
home: the rather sinister Venice of Milly Theale's final agonies
is paralleled, as we shall see, by the enervating Rome of the
biography's conclusion.

Yet the book is "not . . . a biography pure and simple," [9] as
James himself confessed, even though approximately two thirds
of it are quotations from letters by Story and others. Instead it
comprises a richly documented tribute to those nineteenth-century Americans who, as "earlier pilgrims and more candid victims" (I, 5), were among the first to seek nurture in Europe and
especially in Italy for the artistic inclinations that seemed slighted
if not stifled at home. James envies them both their oportunities
and their innocence. He feels they were "just in time for the best
parts of the feast" (I, 8), that "all the discoveries now are made"
(I, 12), and that finally "it has ceased to be feasible . . . to get
away from America" (I, 27): the modern expatriate is "shut out
from a paradise" (I, 97). The documentary aspect involves the
examination of an entire Anglo-American cultural community of
approximately the period 1840 to 1880; the tribute allows James
to utilize "my own little personal memories, inferences, evocations and imaginations," to contrast the Europe he knew with the
Europe of the Story circle.[10] The result, he explained to Mrs.
Story, was a "picture, . . . charming, heterogeneous, and a little
ghostly, of a great cluster of people, a society practically extinct,
with Mr. and Mrs. Story, naturally, all along, the centre, the
pretext, so to.speak, and the *point d'appui.*"[11]

The process of the work as a whole, therefore, is one of both
meditation and mediation. James can at last give full rein to his
romantic propensities; he broods on the past, he revels in it, and
is even prepared to risk the "imputation"

of making a mere Rome of words, talking of a Rome of my own which was no Rome of reality. That comes up as exactly the point— that no Rome of reality was concerned in our experience, that the whole thing was a rare state of the imagination. (II, 209)

James in other words is now precisely balanced between "the passion that fancies" and "that passion that knows"; he willingly admits that romantic Italy never existed, but is nevertheless firmly convinced that "no Rome of reality" is immensely preferable to no Rome at all. Thus in *William Wetmore Story* his stance is alternately indulgent and severe, responding to the "appeal, the ghostly claim . . . of a dislodged, a vanished society" (I, 14) with untiring ardor and tenderness and at the same time calmly appraising its actual accomplishments. As best he can he apologizes for and explains the precursors in question, giving them the full value of their daring and conviction; and finally he judges their experiences, in the person of the "frankly and forcibly romantic" Story (II, 77), as a totality, as an event in the history of American aesthetics and the American consciousness.

This judgment comes toward the close of the second volume and is in every way curious and important, revealing as it does not only James's matured feelings about Italy as a nourisher of the artistic temperament but also his thoughts on the whole problem of expatriation. He begins by claiming that "somehow, in the long-run, Story *paid*—paid for having sought his development even among the circumstances that . . . appeared not alone the most propitious, but the only possible." (Though he adds the demur that "speculations as to what might have been are ever, I know, as futile as they are fascinating"—1903 is also the year of "The Beast in the Jungle.") The sculptor is grouped with "those existences . . . that, in alien air, far from their native soil, have found themselves . . . the prey of mere beguilement"; his career is termed "a sort of beautiful sacrifice to a noble mistake," partially because his "conception of the agreeable as something constant, crude, [and] immediate" involved "an ultimate penalty." Somehow the proper "relation" between creator and subject failed to develop: "The golden air of Rome, we tend to infer, did not make that relation quite intense, quite responsible; partly, no doubt, by taking it too much as a matter of course" (II, 222–5).

This, then, was the danger of Rome and of Italy in general, the danger of an overly facile appeal to the creative powers, of irresponsible aestheticism: the danger, in short, of romance. At this juncture we should be reminded of other American artists ravaged by contact with Italy, of victims like Theobald and Roderick Hudson and even of victimizers like Gilbert Osmond and the narrator of "The Aspern Papers," deluded esthetes all. For James, Story is the reality that proves the fiction and at long last precipitates "the truth I have been feeling my way to," which is that

> the "picturesque" subject, for literary art, has by no means all its advantage in the picturesque country; yields its full taste, gives out *all* its inspiration, in other words, in some air unfriendly to the element at large. I seem, for instance, to see Story gouge . . . from the block of his idea with a finer rage in—let me tell the whole truth—Boston by the Charles, or even in London by the Thames, than in Rome, in Florence. . . . In London, in Boston, he would have *had* to live with his conception, there being nothing else about him of the same colour or quality. In Rome, Florence, Siena, there was too much. . . . Was it not this "too much" therefore that, given the nature of Story's mind . . . constituted precisely, and most characteristically and gracefully, the amusement of wanton Italy at the expense of her victim? (II, 225–6)

The aesthetic doctrine propounded here recalls the Parnassian rigor of Theophile Gautier, a writer James much admired, in his poem "L'Art," which begins:

> Oui, l'oeuvre sort plus belle
> D'une forme au travail
>   Rebelle,
> Vers, marbre, onyx, email.
>
> Point de contraintes fausses!
> Mais que pour marcher droit
>   Tu chausses,
> Muse, un cothurne étroit.[12]

James wants to extend the difficulty we know delighted him to the environment in which creative endeavor takes place, he absolutely requires unsympathetic surroundings; and he also wants to escape the overabundance of suggestiveness that he has come to consider the major drawback of "wanton Italy" for the artist.[13]

Even further, he now sees at least a negative appeal in the aesthetic "American scene" that perhaps prefigures an openness to positive impressions on his return to the States in 1904; and last of all, he is haunted by the idea of what, for Story, a purely American career and development might have resulted in. Is he thinking of himself too—notice the juxtaposition of Boston and London—or simply of American expatriates in general? Such broodings finally assume definite shape in "The Jolly Corner" of 1909; meanwhile, Spencer Brydon's tenacious pursuit of his ghostly alternative is anticipated not just in *William Wetmore Story*'s wholesale evocation of the "visitable past," but even more specifically in such a passage as that on the Bagni di Lucca, where the Palace of Elisa Bonaparte makes James feel "the wave of the feathers and fans, the rattle of the scabbards, the dice, the diplomatic laughter, of a small, old-world Court"—a Court which "affects us as of just the right size to keep rustling away, in a mass, as we follow it; keep swimming, in advance, over the polished floors, with a ghostly click and patter, and, through whatever door we enter, whisking out of sight by the opposite" (I, 278). In *The American Scene* and "The Jolly Corner" and the autobiographical books of his last years, James finally overtook his ghosts; but the attempt, and the specific process, began in *William Wetmore Story*.[14]

III

The Golden Bowl (1904) is the culminating work of James's career as a writer of fiction, both his last major novel and his last extended treatment of the international situation, the lover's quarrel between Europe and America. The work has yet another unique distinction: its Italian Prince is the only continental European in the entire Jamesian canon who is depicted from the inside, the only character neither American nor English that James ever "goes behind." The original Notebook entry of November 28, 1892 posited the young hero as French, and the reasons for the decision to make him Italian are unknown;[15] the result, however, is a gathering together of all James's Italian themes into final consummate expression. Yet they have been so thoroughly merged with larger concerns that to trace them adequately the novel must be examined as a whole, even if much of the discussion seems at first irrelevant, for only then can we understand how profoundly Amerigo's nationality affects its ultimate significance.

That significance has eluded many of its readers. *The Golden Bowl* "is the large problem child among James's writings," says F. W. Dupee: "How did he intend us to feel about the Ververs, father and daughter?"[16] It is indeed easy to find them morally obtuse, the father especially, since James leaves us in no doubt that he has literally purchased Prince Amerigo for his daughter; "You're at any rate a part of his collection," she complacently remarks to her fiancé in the opening chapter.[17] Adam subsequently compounds his original purchase and himself marries

Charlotte Stant, not because he is in love with her, but to prevent Maggie from thinking he feels abandoned. The obverse of this tender altruism is a strange callousness: Adam apparently considers Charlotte and Amerigo only as objects, as products of his own inimitable alchemy. Certainly the Ververs so take for granted their complete possession that they totally neglect the necessary "upkeep." As a result Charlotte and Amerigo become lovers, and here it is tempting to see them as perfectly justified in asserting their independence of the pattern into which Adam's wealth and Maggie's indifference have placed them.

In the end, however, father and daughter triumph together and the adulterers are separated, though it is impossible not to wonder by what right Maggie reclaims her husband, after having made his offense almost inevitable, and at the same time deprives Charlotte not only of the Prince but of her very freedom. *The Golden Bowl* can be viewed, then, as a study of two ingenuously evil Americans who, backed by the power of enormous wealth, ruin the lives of their respective spouses first through ignorance and then through ruthless coercion. But in actuality it is even less a simple tale of victims and victimizers than *The Wings of the Dove,* offering instead a complex tangle of guilt and innocence to which no single person holds the moral clue. The interaction of its four major characters thus counts for everything, though in order to judge them collectively it is first necessary to consider them as individuals.

Adam Verver's position in the circumscribed world of the novel is seemingly that of patriarch, but the specific role he plays eludes easy description. There is something vague about his dominance: we know he controls but seldom see him controlling, we realize he is powerful but rarely see his power in action. He is perhaps an unconvincing portrayal of a self-made millionaire,

too bland and indecisive, too "modest" and "simple," but if he
lacks the assertiveness of the empire builder, it must be remembered that his empires are behind him; they have been made, and
have made him, long before the book opens. We see him only
in retirement, as a man of taste, "one of the great collectors of
the world" (I, 100) and at first glance this might seem an unlikely
transformation for what we must suppose was once a hardheaded
tycoon on the order of Jay Gould. But Adam actually applies his
energies to collecting art as methodically and efficiently as if he
were making his fortune all over again. "To rifle the Golden Isles
had become . . . the business of his future" (I, 141), says James
with unmistakable irony; assuming he brings to his new interest
all the taste and sincerity one could expect of a cultivated American, his methods remain those of a plutocrat. He has nothing to
give but what he can amass, and to build his museum in American
City, fervidly projected as "positively civilization condensed, con-
crete, consummate, set down by his hands as a house on a rock"
(I, 145), he dismantles Europe without stopping to assimilate it,
as Yankee millionaires once moved English abbeys piecemeal
and set them up on incongruous California hillsides. Art to him
is a product, not a process; his sensibility is literally conservative,
informing without upsetting the life he now lives:

> It was at bottom, with him, the aesthetic principle, planted where
> it could burn with a cold, still flame; . . . where, in short, in spite
> of the general tendency of the "devouring element" to spread, the
> rest of his spiritual furniture, modest, scattered, and tended with
> unconscious care, escaped the consumption that in so many cases
> proceeds from the undue keeping-up of profane altar-fires. Adam
> Verver had in other words learnt the lesson of the senses, to the
> end of his own little book, without having for a day raised the
> smallest scandal in his economy at large. (I, 197)

"The lesson of the senses" here is as rigorously budgeted and
categorized as the entries in a ledger. The imagery in this passage

demonstrates the link between Adam's financial acumen and his feeling for art—the latter has simply been substituted for the former. His new enthusiasm is pursued intelligently but unimaginatively; he lacks Gilbert Osmond's sadistic egoism, but the two men share a collector's passion for acquistion without surprises. The significant feature of Adam's ethical diffidence is not that he treats Amerigo as a trophy, but that he simply cannot imagine that the Prince will ever have to change. A work of art, after all, is a constant, and is not the Prince a superlative work of art? It is here that we find his essential failing: the museum world he has so carefully assembled has no accommodating flexibility. His gold supports Amerigo and Charlotte at the same time that his static morality stifles them; they fit so neatly and balance each other so exactly that Adam as their curator must suppose them perfectly happy because perfectly displayed.

Yet though in general complacently unaware, he is on at least one occasion fleetingly troubled by the idyllic felicity he and Maggie enjoy with such a conspicuous lack of effort: "Well, we're tremendously moral for ourselves—that is for each other; and I won't pretend that I know at whose particular personal expense you and I, for instance, are happy" (II, 92). But he is not able to move beyond this vague sense of indebtedness which oddly implies that happiness is some form of capitalistic exploitation. He does not "pretend" to know, and one may assume that he does not intend to know; but what is nearly certain is that there are some things he cannot know. Adam, in fact, is as incapable of change as the art he collects; throughout the novel he never adjusts to circumstances but instead adjusts circumstances to fit him. His manipulation of others is curiously childlike; he is frequently compared to a "little boy" (I, 324) and seems impervious to the claims of mature moral responsibility. His mystery like Christina Light's is one of unfathomable innocence: he is "inscrutable" and, Fanny Assingham speculates, "he may be stupid too" (II, 135)—the two qualities are perhaps complementary.

Charlotte curiously enough shows disabilities similar to those of her husband. Her moral capacity too is strictly limited; she is the prime mover of the novel's Italianate conspiracy and yet hardly considers herself accountable for instigating it, for she supposedly enters into marriage with Adam and its dangerous proximity to the Prince only after the most scrupulous soul-searching—"there were beautiful intentions all round" (I, 392), says Fanny, thus providing the ironic epigraph for much of James's later fiction. But it is hard to believe she utterly discounts the risk involved and far more likely that she simply feels herself superior to the entire situation and fully prepared to deal with its difficulties. Certainly she is by no means in love with Adam. Her rational and slightly chilling approach is the complement of his own: in the end he buys only what she is perfectly willing to sell. She is, in short, an adventuress, but no common one. Charlotte is the perfect social animal; everyone in the novel praises her as "a rare, a special product" (I, 54) and basks in the brilliance of her "grand style" and "tested facility" (I, 317). She evinces the carnal vitality that attracted Merton Densher to Kate Croy, the worldly glamor of the Princess Casamassima; "life is somehow becoming to her," as James remarked of an earlier heroine.[18] Like Madame Merle and Gilbert Osmond, Charlotte is an impoverished expatriate American, at home in Europe and eager for wealth. These factors account for both her suave cosmopolitanism and her aggressive outlook: she resents her deprivation and is confident of her ability to overcome it. Life to her is a challenge, almost an obstacle, and her most splendid accomplishment is that of playing her difficult cards with insouciant skill while at the same time enjoying the game.

Yet life is perhaps in her case too exciting, the game too thrilling, or more precisely, the thrills are too gratuitous, for Charlotte not only takes risks when given the chance, she coolly seeks them out on her own. She manages the details of the adultery with an unruffled expertise that even affects Amerigo now and then as a species of brutality. When at one point she covertly jeers at him for being afraid, he confesses "I'm only afraid of *you*, a little, at moments" (I, 340), and he has good reason to be: Charlotte is a formidable woman, and is proud of the fact. Her pride, indeed, is one of her most salient characteristics and tends to express itself with a sinister luxuriance. Just after her marriage, for example, she is glimpsed in haughty isolation at a "great official party," "crowned" with "unsurpassed diamonds" under "a dome of lustres," her "high tiara, her folded fan, her indifferent, unattended eminence" as conspicuous as her sense of being "supremely justified" (I, 246–8). This is reminiscent of the "exalted" Satan of *Paradise Lost,* "High on a throne of royal state, . . . by merit raised / To that bad eminence" (II, 1–6); the two scenes share the same "eminence," the same lush pageantry and insolent infernal pride. Charlotte feels exhilarated by her beauty, her wealth, but above all by her power: she is playing the game magnificently, and what is better, she now makes the rules.

But she reveals the fatal flaw in her experiment with living when she remarks to the Prince, "Ah, for things I mayn't want to know, I promise you shall find me stupid" (I, 363). This means that Charlotte, for all her fine flexibility, cannot adjust her pride to circumstances that require an admission of ignorance. Thus her misery at Fawns, when she roams like a wild beast escaped from its "cage," is largely self-inflicted; she will not, she cannot seek recourse from anyone, since to do so would be to admit failure. When Maggie approaches her, Charlotte's instinctive reaction is a retreat into dissimulation and disdain: "Pride, indeed, the next moment, had become the mantle caught up for protection and perversity; she flung it round her as a denial of any loss of her freedom" (II, 313).

Such a gesture, however, only condemns her to further subjection. The ultimate drawback of her supreme self-confidence is that she can only proceed as if she were frustrated, never as if she had made a mistake. Life is a game she can only play offensively; experience at first stimulates, but finally baffles her, for she cannot let it alter the fixed idea of her triumphant superiority. "She's stupid" (II, 348), says the Prince toward the end of the novel, echoing her earlier judgment on herself; and her pride, ironically, is at once the source of her stupidity and its means of preservation.[19]

In contrast to her father and stepmother, Maggie Verver shows a genuine capacity for change; her transition from opaque innocence to enlightened experience is the only significant development in any of the novel's characters, and, rightly understood, demonstrates the complete interdependence of knowledge and morality in later Jamesian fiction.[20] Our initial glimpse of her on the eve of her marriage, however, reveals a moderately intelligent, modestly attractive young girl whose exposure to Europe has done little to counteract her basic American naiveté. What is impressive at this point is her astounding combination of innocence and insensitivity; she has not been so much spoiled by enormous wealth as dulled by it. Her indifference to complexities is systematic: she simply refuses to recognize certain sides of life, for she has so sedulously adopted her father's attitudes that she cannot begin to question their value, much less the man behind them. She has learned her lesson well, and it has been above all a lesson in economics. Freedom from want paradoxically commits her to a rigid, unimaginative existence where everything has a price and people are evaluated like shares on a moral stock market; this is the impetus behind her determination to compensate Adam for whatever her marriage may have "cost" him. In her view, apparently, as in his, a limited amount of emotional currency backs every human relation and exact change must be returned, spouse for spouse, Charlotte for Amerigo. The Ververs' mutual concern is often very touching, but surely has the distinct air of rather over-cautious transactions between two unsmiling businessmen.

We further learn in our first view of Maggie her motive for marrying the Prince: "It wasn't," she tells him, "your particular self. It was the generations behind you, the follies and the crimes, the plunder and the waste—the wicked Pope, the monster most of all. . . . Where, therefore . . . without your archives, annals, infamies, would you have been?" (I, 9–10). This should remind us of Miss Gunton of Poughkeepsie, who also loved an Italian Prince for his archives; Amerigo is the last in a long Jamesian series of Italians who are paid by Americans to be colorful, unusual, picturesque—in a word, romantic. In the beginning was the poor venal Vicenza family of "Travelling Companions," then the fugitive Signora of "At Isella," Serafina and Conte Valerio, Miss Gunton's Prince, Eugenio, and finally Amerigo. There is in the end hardly any other sort of Italian in Jamesian fiction, for the good reason that nearly all his Americans in Italy are both wealthy and yearning to be deluded. Amerigo indeed remarks to his fiancée that "you Americans are almost incredibly romantic," to which Maggie answers:

> "Of course we are. That's just what makes everything so nice for us."
> "Everything?" He had wondered.
> "Well, everything that's nice at all. The world, the beautiful world —or everything in it that *is* beautiful. I mean we see so much."

He had looked at her a moment. . . . But what he had answered was: "You see too much—that's what may sometimes make you difficulties. When you don't, at least," he had amended with a further thought, "see too little."

Amerigo supposes that the Ververs are immune to "the follies of the romantic disposition" (I, 11), but on the contrary James surely intends them to demonstrate the unhealthiness of romanticism even at its least passionate. For the Ververs are romantics only in the sense that they make life easier for themselves by simplifying it along aesthetic lines; their "romanticism" is not just a distortion, but an evasion of life, a surrogate that somehow takes the place of active struggle, suffering, knowledge. Its appeal is exactly that it is only "nice," that it makes no demands, that it feeds on sentiment as opposed to real experience. Maggie at the opening of the novel is an innocent romantic possessed of a blind faith in the goodness of life and of the people around her. In Fanny's words, she "wasn't born to know evil. She must never know it" (I, 78)—not because it is too ugly or violent but because it is complex, it is difficult to understand.

This is the Maggie Verver who says to her father in the garden at Fawns, "I don't *want* to know!" (I, 187) and insists that "I live in terror. . . . I'm a small creeping thing" (I, 181), and this is the only Maggie we see until she abruptly awakens to the conspiracy that Amerigo and Charlotte have formed against her. The realization is a shock: she feels "arranged apart" and sees for the first time that her own arrangements can be, in fact have been, rejected as arbitrary. But at this point she makes the gratuitous decision on which the novel pivots, that she loves Amerigo deeply and must win him back, and on the basis of this assumption she finds herself committed to strange new values. The very basis of the intrigue between her husband and stepmother is her own continued ignorance of it; yet now, vitalized by her sense of crisis and half afraid of what she may learn, she suddenly wants to know everything:

> Knowledge, knowledge, was a fascination as well as a fear; and a part precisely of the strangeness of this juncture was the way her apprehension that [Amerigo] would break out to her with some merely general profession was mixed with her dire need to forgive him, to reassure him, to respond to him, on no ground that she didn't fully measure. (II, 140)

Maggie's habitual "terror," in other words, is overcome by her "need" to "measure"; she lives her "knowledge" so intensely that she discovers "a fascination as well as a fear" in watching Amerigo anxiously for "any change of surface, any difference of expression or intention." And James continues:

> There had been, through life, as we know, few quarters in which the Princess's fancy could let itself loose; but it shook off restraint when it plunged into the figured void of the detail of that relation. This was a realm it could people with images—again and again with fresh ones; they swarmed there like the strange combinations that lurked in the woods at twilight; they loomed into the definite and faded into the vague, their main present sign for her being however that they were always, that they were duskily, agitated. (II, 280)

What has happened is that "abject" little Maggie, as she is so frequently called,[21] at last finds her life genuinely, absorbingly romantic. What she now experiences is not the romanticized escapism of her relationship with Adam, but instead the *passion* that fancies, or what might be called the romance of involvement. For the first time in James's fiction, apart from isolated incidents like Isabel Archer's Roman wanderings, Sacred and Profane Love are blended rather than juxtaposed, allowed to combine rather than combat: Maggie visualizes an exotic pagoda and a desert caravan, she imagines herself "thrown over on her back with her neck . . . half-broken and her helpless face staring up" (II, 242) or as "some Indian squaw with a papoose on her back and barbarous beadwork to sell" (II, 323–4). And yet this romantic sense of her dilemma is completely justified by the circumstances, for it is not irresponsible invention but imaginative conception, not mere fancy but valid analogy.

This is especially true of the most persistent vein of imagery she employs. Since Maggie is both the wife of an Italian and a woman engaged in Italianate intrigue, she understandably tends to equate the conspiratorial with the theatrical. At first she sees herself as "an actress who had been studying a part and rehearsing it, but who suddenly, on the stage, before the footlights, had begun to improvise, to speak lines not in the text" (II, 33). Later she is "the lady in short spangled skirts" made to "caper and posture" at the circus (II, 71), or feels like

> some young woman of the theatre who, engaged for a minor part in the play and having mastered her cues with anxious effort, should find herself suddenly promoted to leading lady and expected to appear in every act of the five. (II, 208)

Her attempt to regain the Prince is like that of "some panting dancer of a difficult step who had capered, before the footlights of an empty theatre, to a spectator lounging in a box" (II, 222); she experiences the fatigue of "a tired actress who has the good fortune to be 'off ' " (II, 231) and of an "overworked little trapezist girl" (II, 302). Once she goes even further, and imagines the conversations and unspoken thoughts of Amerigo, Charlotte and her father, whom she sees as "figures rehearsing some play of which she herself was the author" (II, 235). Though such an attitude may seem dangerously manipulative, the comparison is apt. By the sheer energy of her imagination Maggie fuses reality and romance without sacrificing the validity of the former or the vividness of the latter; her love for Amerigo brings her life, her personality, her sensibility out of the wings and onto the stage.

But Maggie not only learns to love intensely and imaginatively; she also, perhaps paradoxically, learns to spare, becoming James's most memorable illustration of the heroism of inaction, a growing concern of the Major Phase and to some extent an interiorized version of the traditionally supreme kingly virtue of clemency. Thus she wisely leaves Amerigo alone to determine his salvation "on *his* terms, not at all on hers" (II, 322), she pretends to Adam that nothing is changed, "making his protect-edness . . . still the law of her attitude and the key to her solu-tion" (II, 163), she humbles herself before her stepmother and renounces the very vindictiveness of which she allows Charlotte to accuse her. For retribution is nothing to Maggie while restitu-tion is everything. She wants "the golden bowl—as it *was* to have been" (II, 216), the ideal love she once in ignorance thought was already hers. Maggie determines to know, Maggie changes, Mag-gie triumphs, and through it all she masks her inner tumult with a studied and selfless impassivity. "I'm not extraordinary," she says to Fanny Assingham, "but I *am,* for every one, quiet" (II, 217).

But she is not able to know everything. Her shortcomings are the obverse of her particular virtues; just as romanticism and spontaneity and love illuminate her purpose, they are also poten-tial falsifications of it. It is love that dominates Maggie, and love blinds her to the full truth. At the end of the novel, although she realizes she must abandon her father, she still does not see him as inadvertently sinister and a determining factor in both her own ignorance and Charlotte and Amerigo's adultery. She tells Fanny that she and Adam are "lost to each other really much more than Amerigo and Charlotte are; since for them it's just, it's right, it's deserved, while for us it's only sad and strange and not caused by our fault" (II, 333). And as if this were not sanctimonious enough, in the novel's final scene she can still admire her father's "note of possession and control" (II, 365). Love may sacrifice but does not repudiate; she will give Adam up because she knows it is necessary but she will never deny him, and for the same reason she will never take revenge on Charlotte and Amerigo. Maggie in short will never fully comprehend the darkness of human motives because her will to win transforms so much of it into dazzling and misleading light. She confronts evil at such close quarters that she cannot see her own face reflected in its eyes, she cannot see the quantity of self-indulgence in her abjection or the unexamined elements in her morality. She and Adam are of course as responsible as Amerigo and Charlotte for what has happened, but a complete recognition of this will always elude her; strong as is her desire for knowledge, her need to feel completely justified is stronger still.

Yet after all Maggie earns her success even if she does not wholly deserve it. She suffers agonies so overwhelming she can hardly find names for them: on the one hand, the horror of calling treachery by domestic names, of "finding evil seated, all at its ease, where she had only dreamed of good" (II, 237), and on the other, the daily suppressions and dissimulations, the sudden fears that must be stifled, the trembling that must be controlled—all the necessary restraints of heroic inaction, of keeping one's romantic life purely imaginative and interior. She often feels that such moments are unbearable and yet she bears them, at one point thinking of herself as "some far-off harassed heroine —only with a part to play for which she knew, exactly, no inspiring precedent" (II, 307). The very "precedent" she lacks, however, is eventually defined by her ordeal, and it is a magnificent one.

But Maggie must not be taken as embodying the moral meaning of *The Golden Bowl*, since even at its conclusion she is only partially aware of what she has done and why. What is certain is that she has done it primarily for the Prince: he is the original purchase, the object of rival affections and the justification of Maggie's triumph, and if she is regarded as the novel's chief protagonist, and he is made its center of gravity, its full significance becomes clearer.

The Prince is doubly unique in James's fiction, at once his most carefully and fully developed European character and the most extended and profound expression of what he understood Italy and the Italian ethos to be.[22] What first strikes us about him is a flexibility as inveterate as it is sometimes disturbing. He wholly lacks Maggie's moralistic pugnacity and Charlotte's isolating pride; the ambition to command and control is utterly foreign to his "passive and prudent" nature. He is, as Adam says, "variously and inexhaustibly round" (I, 138), and the one lesson in life he has learned supremely well is to accept events rather than attempt to direct them. "The Prince had always liked his London," reads the opening sentence of the novel, "when it had come to him": a conspicuous exponent of *dolce far niente*, he does nothing with such instinctive elegance that the Ververs understandably conceive of him in decorative terms. "You're a rarity, an object of beauty, an object of price" (I, 12), Maggie tells him; he appeals to Adam as "a representative precious object" (I, 140). Like Camillo Conte Valerio he is a beautifully finished product of an ancient civilization, and the heritage of centuries has done so little to burden him and so much to polish him that he seems almost unnaturally amenable. Life for him is a pageant that one watches when it is interesting and ignores when one is bored, and because of his noble birth and his marriage to Maggie, he can enjoy this spectacle to the highest advantage. Moreover, as a perfect, perceptive, unhurried observer of existence and of himself, he assiduously cultivates the luxuries of introspection, but is never so gauche as to brood; yielding to tortuous soul-searching would be ungentlemanly, and Amerigo is superlatively a gentleman.

It is indeed of the utmost importance that his code forbids him, in every situation, to act as anything less than a *galantuomo,* and that his standards of gallantry are strictly Italian rather than American. He commits adultery, for instance, only when it becomes clear that his wife and father-in-law are too involved with each other to notice or care. He is not hoodwinked by Charlotte's rationalizations, and is properly skeptical of "their having plotted so very hard against their destiny" (I, 289). On the other hand he feels required "not to be too eminent a fool" (I, 310) and fiercely resents the absurd position in which Maggie has unwittingly placed him:

> Being thrust, systematically, with another woman, and a woman one happened, by the same token, exceedingly to like, and being so thrust that the theory of it seemed to publish one as idiotic or incapable—this was a predicament of which the dignity depended all on one's own handling. What was supremely grotesque in fact was the essential opposition of theories—as if a galantuomo, as *he* at least constitutionally conceived galantuomini, could do anything but blush to "go about" at such a rate with such a person as Mrs. Verver in a state of childlike innocence, the state of our primitive parents before the Fall. (I, 334)

It is one of James's masterstrokes that Amerigo interprets Maggie's unquestioning confidence in him as an insult to his masculinity; given their "opposition of theories," though, he can hardly do otherwise. The "dignity" of a gentleman, obviously, is not a matter of ethical absolutes but rather the art of mediating conflicts between pleasure and self-respect, or as the Prince defines it, "doing the best for one's self one can—without injury to others" (I, 58). His pragmatic code tells him that a gentleman never inflicts pain, and since a discreet sexual intrigue could not hurt Maggie, while a repudiation of it would definitely affront Charlotte, he decides to accept the situation—and for the Prince, to accept is to act.

Yet to describe him only as a graceful hedonist would be to make him as static as Charlotte or Adam. Amerigo is not at all self-satisfied in his detachment and inaction: one of his most engaging characteristics is his restless curiosity, his openness to new stimuli. At the beginning of the novel, as he strolls the London streets and contemplates his approaching marriage, he sees that

> he was to constitute a possesion, yet was to escape being reduced to his component parts. What would this mean but that, practically, he was never to be tried or tested? What would it mean but that, if they didn't "change" him, they really wouldn't know—he wouldn't know himself—how many pounds, shillings and pence he had to give? (I, 23)

The point is that the Prince wants to be "tested" by the Ververs. He is "one of the Modern Romans" (I, 3), like his counterpart in "Miss Gunton of Poughkeepsie," and thrills to the thought that "his future *might* be scientific" (I, 17). He feels "somehow full of his race" and yet considers:

> What was this so important step he had just taken but the desire for some new history that should, so far as possible, contradict, and even if need be flatly dishonour, the old? If what had come to him wouldn't do he must *make* something different.

This eagerness for "something different" points to the most attractive of his many virtues, his conscientious "cultivation of humility" (I, 16). He confesses to Fanny Assingham before his marriage: "I'm excellent, I really think, all round—except that

I'm stupid. I can do pretty well anything I *see*. But I've got to see it first. . . . I don't in the least mind it's having to be shown me—in fact I like that better" (I, 30). Amerigo's self-deprecation is in turn related to his "sense of the past" and of how little in himself he can call his own. As he explains to Maggie:

> There are two parts of me . . . one is made up of the history, the doings, the marriages, the crimes, the follies, the boundless *betises* of other people. . . . But there's another part, smaller doubtless, which such as it is, represents my single self, the unknown, unimportant—unimportant save to *you*—personal quantity. About this you've found out nothing. (I, 9)

The Prince, in short, aspires to modernity, he wants to throw off history and become an individual. The Ververs, however, prize him only as an artifact and not for his "single self"; they want to enjoy him possessively and yet passively, as something they own but have no responsibility for. Amerigo honestly wants to understand their values and goals—"he really worked," says James, "poor young man, for acceptance, since he worked so constantly for comprehension" (I, 158)—but the Ververs are conscious of nothing to teach, and the prime reason for his later disillusionment is that

> with these people among whom he was married . . . one found one used one's imagination mainly for wondering how they contrived so little to appeal to it. He felt at moments as if there were never anything to do for them that was worthy—to call worthy—of the personal relation; never any charming charge to take of any confidence deeply reposed. (I, 314)

Thus when the "fresh start" of his marriage leads nowhere and he feels more of an "outsider" than ever, he inevitably turns to Charlotte for comfort:

> You're of the same race . . . the same general tradition and education, of the same moral paste. There are things you have in common with them. But I, on my side, as I've gone on trying to see if I haven't some of these things too—I, on my side, have more and more failed. There seems at last to be nothing worth mentioning. I can't help seeing it—I'm decidedly too different. (I, 310–11)

Amerigo is now convinced that he has "sold himself" (I, 358), that he represents only "the figure of a cheque" (I, 325) to the Ververs. Charlotte capitalizes on his sense of isolation—"we're immensely alone" (I, 308), she tells him—and by the time Maggie recognizes her husband's alienation it is almost too late to retrieve him. He has been morally paralyzed; his desire for new experience is in abeyance and he now thinks only of preserving things as they are, as he and Charlotte now want them. Yet gradually Maggie wins him over. Initially he pities her, next he is interested, finally he is impressed by what she knows, by how much she cares, and not least, by the success with which she manages to resist him.

For the Prince, it must be stressed, is not used to being resisted by women: quite the contrary. If his most attractive virtue is humility, his most compelling attraction is his sexuality, and its importance in *The Golden Bowl* makes him an anomaly among Jamesian heroes. He distills the essence of the carnal appeal James sensed in Italy and in Italians like the Conte Valerio and Angelo Beati; Prince Amerigo is not merely handsome and suave but the principle of maleness embodied. Early in the novel we are told that "the Prince's notion of a recompense to women . . . was more or less to make love to them" (I, 21–2), and when Charlotte returns to London he ponders, "as a man conscious of having known many women,"

> the recurrent, the predestined phenomenon . . . the doing by the woman of the thing that gave her away. She did it, ever, inevitably,

infallibly—she couldn't possibly not do it. It was her nature, it was her life, and the man could always expect it without lifting a finger. This was *his*, the man's, any man's, position and strength—that he had necessarily the advantage, that he had only to wait with a decent patience to be placed, it might really be said, in the right. Just so the punctuality of performance on the part of the other creature was her weakness and her deep misfortune—not less, no doubt, than her beauty. It produced for the man that extraordinary mixture of pity and profit in which his relation with her, when he was not a mere brute, mainly consisted; and gave him in fact his most pertinent ground of being nice to her, nice about her, nice *for* her. (I, 49–50)

In this passage the Prince recognizes his immense power and also a need to restrain it, to be merciful. His attitude is both compassionate and a bit smug; that he could ever be at the mercy of women is inconceivable, since in his eyes they are doomed to perpetual "abjection." Maggie herself, the one woman who, in a sense, defies his supremacy, also demonstrates how this notably sensual man inspires notable sensuality in others. Her physical response to Amerigo has all the intensity of intoxication; upon his return from Matcham "the plenitude of his presence" affects her, in a burst of orgasmic imagery, as a "warmly-washing wave": "She had subsequently lived for hours she couldn't count under the dizzying smothering welter—positively in submarine depths where everything came to her through walls of emerald and mother-of-pearl" (II, 42–3).

But Maggie's recent suspicions now show her the danger of being "in his power" (II, 28). She feels that to regain him she must not surrender herself so easily, and one night as they are riding home in their carriage he applies "the infinite pressure of her whole person to his own" only to find her "immensely resisting." She realizes that he wants her to give over her plan: "it was exactly for this that he had resorted to unfailing magic. He *knew how* to resort to it—he could be, on occasion, as she had lately more than ever learned, so munificent a lover" (II, 56). Yet Maggie perseveres, despite her "tears of suffered pain" (II, 57). This must be a novel experience for the Prince, and we must assume that he respects his wife's heroic defense. They both know, however, that eventually she must yield to his "sovereign personal power" (II, 139); he says as much when towards the end of the novel he tells her to "wait . . . till they've gone. Till they're away . . . Till we're really alone." Amerigo has no need to be explicit, since at this point Maggie is seized by an overwhelming "terror of her endless power of surrender":

> He was so near now that she could touch him, taste him, smell him, kiss him, hold him; he almost pressed upon her, and the warmth of his face—frowning, smiling, she mightn't know which; only beautiful and strange—was bent upon her with the largeness with which objects loom in dreams. (II, 351–2)

The voluptuously detailed eroticism of this passage is unparalleled in James; it posits Amerigo as a presence of irresistible sensuousness and virility.[23] Maggie on this occasion fends him off again, but only until Adam and Charlotte have left. By the last page she is back in his arms, "his whole act enclosing her" (II, 369), and if anything is definite at the conclusion of *The Golden Bowl*, it is that the Prince will now keep his promise.

But we should understand that this promise is not a matter of "mere zoological sociability"; the implications of such an ending for the novel as a whole are profound. If Maggie displays a dangerous moral complacency, if she tends like her father to see people as objects and to manipulate them, the Prince is both an obstacle she cannot surmount and her personal salvation. He is the one person in the novel beyond her control; she is in some sense answerable to him, to the domination of his sexuality, of

her need for it. Her devotion to Adam may be the "paramount
law" (II, 203) of her life, but her love for Amerigo is not subject
to legislation, it is outside any moral system, it is simply there.
Thus the power she wields over others finds its limit in his power
over her; the knowledge she uses to triumph is balanced, human-
ized even, by the instinctive passion that Amerigo so effectively
arouses and represents.

The Prince in fact is Maggie's counterpart and complement
throughout the novel. He is the first to be disillusioned by the
outcome of their international marriage, and when his wife confronts him with what she "knows" about the golden bowl, he
suddenly finds, as she has done, that their relationship is drasti-
cally altered: "No, he had used her, he had even exceedingly
enjoyed her, before this; but there had been no precedent for
that character of a proved necessity to him which she was rapidly
taking on" (II, 186). Amerigo subsequently acts out the solitary
torment that Maggie has already endured:

> He was walking ostensibly beside her, but was in fact given over to
> the grey medium in which he helplessly groped; a perception on
> her part which was a perpetual pang and which might last what it
> would—for ever if need be—but which if relieved at all must be
> relieved by his act alone. (II, 281)

He is "a proud man in abjection" (II, 228), and "abject" is a word
peculiarly associated with Maggie; he like her must create a new
life in the "prison" of "his own act and his own choice" (II, 338).
Yet finally he makes his decision, and Maggie quickly senses that
"he was with her as if he were hers, hers in a degree and on a
scale, with an intensity and an intimacy, that were a new and a
strange quantity" (II, 339). And she begins really for the first time
to understand the man she will soon be "alone" with: "it came

over her that he had after all a simplicity, very considerable, on which she had never dared to presume" (II, 344).

The Prince may in truth be simple, but his simplicity is not the sort that simplifies. He is aware of complexity but keeps himself aloof from it; there is a certain shadow over his usually eager response to experience that becomes apparent now and then in an admonitory stance or abrupt withdrawal. He is, to begin with, superstitious: it should be remembered that he refuses to buy the golden bowl because he is sure it will bring bad luck, and luck itself is for him "that word of unpermitted presumption" (I, 342). But superstition has still deeper roots in his character. The fact is that he enjoys life but does not wholly trust it, and his acceptance of it is always tempered by a somber sense of its inexplicable mystery and tragic potential. Whether his passivity is a cause or an effect of this outlook, it is certain that the two complement and perpetuate each other; Amerigo is a "congruous whole" (I, 328) in that he refuses to pretend even to himself that the struggle aught availeth. He is, in short, a classic Italian fatalist, and his fatalism renders him constitutionally incapable of initial action and constantly alert to the abyss of irony that yawns beneath all human endeavor. He is vision without motivation; he sees, and he sees too much, because he does little else but look. He is too practical to be unhappy, but he is too alone in his knowledge to be completely content. We see him at one juncture letting his "native gaiety go in outbreaks of song, or even of quite whimsical senseless sound, either expressive of intimate relaxation or else fantastically plaintive" (I, 164). Here, we feel, is an attempt to escape through incoherence a pattern only too coherent; here is a man who knows more than he says and wishes he knew less.

Indeed, the novel's four main characters strikingly manifest James's abiding concern with the various imbalances and distortions of Sacred and Profane Love, knowing and fancying, experience and sentiment, reality and romance. In Adam we see experience without fancy, which means that there are things he is incapable of knowing because he literally cannot imagine them, while in Charlotte, as in Gilbert Osmond and Christina Light, knowledge depends directly on a deluded romanticism, on an idealized self-image that is totally resistant to change. Maggie, by contrast, at first does not want to know, but later confronts both reality and romance at the crisis of her life and proceeds to combine and fuse them with a success unique in Jamesian fiction; but she experiences without completely understanding her motivations and cannot properly authorize what she does. The Prince, finally, who sees most of all, is so appalled by an excess of knowledge that his fancy is immobilized: he experiences without hope, and thus lacks the will to act—unless, that is, someone can make him want to, can act for him as it were. This is finally what Maggie alone is able to do; but Amerigo is the only person who can both justify Maggie's endeavors and adequately judge them, which he does when from the depths of his comprehension he tells her: "everything's terrible, cara, in the heart of man" (II, 349). Such a statement contains the essence of James's special vision in *The Golden Bowl*. Amerigo speaks of the human heart as "terrible," yet the grim generalization is broken in two, and thus qualified, by a single word of particular tenderness—"cara."

The same ambiguity appears in the novel's last paragraph after Maggie tells the Prince that Charlotte's being "splendid" is "our help, you see":

> It kept him before her therefore, taking in—or trying to—what she so wonderfully gave. He tried, too clearly, to please her—to meet her in her own way; but with the result only that, close to her, her face kept before him, his hands holding her shoulders, his whole act enclosing her, he presently echoed: " 'See'? I see nothing but *you.*" And the truth of it had with this force after a moment so

strangely lighted his eyes that as for pity and dread of them she buried her own in his breast. (II, 368–9)

Like their relationship as a whole, this final view of Maggie and the Prince partakes of both triumph and tragedy. Amerigo "sees nothing but" his wife because at this very moment his physical need of her is intense as never before, but also because she has carefully eliminated the two other people that stood between them; "the truth" that Maggie glimpses in her husband's eyes is both the desolation she has wrought and the resulting isolation that now binds them together. Yet "pity and dread"—the very formula of Aristotelean purgation—act not to separate them but to further include her in his embrace. His awareness of the evil that taints even Maggie, of the selfishness at the heart of her selflessness, does not lessen his desire for her; Maggie's sense of what she has done is enfolded by a new sense of what there is still to do. In *The Golden Bowl* the long crisis-laden love affair between innocent America and romantic Italy is consummated in a marriage that challenges the deepest energies of both parties. The Prince is a real man worth being "romantic" about: Maggie must learn to live with the profound "simplicity" of his sensuous pessimism even as he must try to fathom her passionate moralism and teach her to temper its excesses.

For the final tableau of *The Golden Bowl* is in essence a significant reverse of the Vicenza episode in James's first Italian tale, "Travelling Companions." [24] There, an American philosophically accepts Italian duplicity as the price one pays for romantic stimulation; over thirty years later, a fatalistic Italian embraces America's distorting romanticism as the necessary concomitant of its idealistic ardor. The first scene has the effect of truce, the second of genuine reconciliation. If, as Christof Wegelin says, "the subject of the novel is the gradual coalescence of Maggie's

and the Prince's moral consciousness," [25] the two of them finally
form "a congruous whole": he has all the depth of his vision and
she has all the breadth of her love, he knows the heart of man
and she perhaps embodies its terror and wonder. They complete
each other, and their ultimate embrace is a spiritual as well as
physical fulfillment, a fusion of knowledge and fancy, Europe and
America. But what does James mean when he shows the Prince
and Princess dividing a world between them? He might be saying
that man's "terrible" fate is to exist amid conditions and act by
motives which, if fully understood, would paralyze his ability to
change, that unbiased knowledge is incompatible with living a life
to any purpose. Only the Sacred and Profane together, only
instinctive action and partially enlightened love can sustain and
save us from the darkness of our egotism and pride, but to do
so they must utilize that darkness and call it light, they must be
selfish in order to be effective. If *The Golden Bowl* tells us that one
must act, but that evil is a part of every action, then its vision is
essentially tragic. Yet obviously the tragedy is qualified by certain
consolations. Though the Prince and Maggie as individuals are
alone and incomplete, at the end of the novel they are together,
they are about to make love; we may therefore suppose that their
bodies will help reconcile them to the "pity and dread" of their
situation, and that together their knowledge is somehow greater
than it is apart.

IV

From April to July 1907 Henry James traveled in Italy, which
impressed him anew, he wrote Edith Wharton upon his return,
as "the most beautiful country in the world—of a beauty (and an

interest and complexity of beauty) so far beyond any other that none other is worth talking about." This was his last visit there, as he himself foresaw: "I have drunk and turned the glass upside down—or rather I have placed it under my heel and smashed it—and the Gipsy life *with* it—for ever." [26]

In 1909 he published *Italian Hours,* an illustrated collection of all his travel articles on Italy. The earlier writings were carefully revised, and James added a "postscript" [27] of four brief essays based on his most recent impressions. These last words on the subject exude a melancholy that some irresistible process has transformed into serene joy by the end of the book. The Master is in his sixties and feels even older: he is "the brooding analyst," the "musing *mature* visitor," the representative of a "remote and romantic tradition" living in a "changed world" where Rome has been "vulgarised" and "cockneyfication" is rife. He seeks to "re-mount the stream of time" (453),[28] to trace "a continuity with the irrecoverable but still effective past" (457), and suddenly, magically, the "life-long victim of Italy" feels "almost verily as never before, the operation of the old love-philtre" (310). The "defiant miracle of life and beauty" (372) once again works its spell; Italy after all has not been exhausted.

The "nest of darknesses," for example, still stirs occasionally, albeit not with its former vigor: at Villa d'Este James gives rein to "my sense of the sinister too, of that vague after-taste as of evil things that lurks so often, for a suspicious sensibility, wherever the terrible game of the life of the Renaissance was played as the Italians played it" (308). Similarly, the landscape near Siena appears as "a great heaving region stilled by some final shock and returning thoughtfully, in fact tragically, on itself" (369). For the most part, though, the pessimism of the Italian emotion has evaporated, leaving only the sensuous elements behind. James rejoices for the last time in the "charmingly civilized"

Italian people, and while touring Tuscany in the summer heat, he has

> the sense of a supremely intimate revelation of Italy in undress, so to speak (the state, it seemed, in which one would most fondly, most ideally, enjoy her); Italy no longer in winter starch and sobriety, with winter manners and winter prices and winter excuses, all addressed to the *forestieri* and the philistines; but lolling at her length, with her graces all relaxed, and thereby only the more natural; the brilliant performer, in short, *en famille,* the curtain down and her salary stopped for the season—thanks to which she is by so much more the easy genius and the good creature as she is by so much less the advertised *prima donna.* (459)

The note of sensuality and theatricalism was never more genially sounded; only Italy, after all, could inspire James to write a lady friend, as he did from Venice in 1907, that because of hot weather, "I have no more clothes to take off." [29]

The ultimate effect of *Italian Hours,* then, is one of "serenity," of "a reconciling . . . an altogether penetrating, last hour" (317). James is delighted with a "two motor-days' feast of scenery" (501) and offers a cautious panegyric to the age of the automobile; he is so moved by Posilippo that he finally yields to the temptation he often rebuked in his fiction, and talks of how "the Italian scene on such occasions as this seems to purify itself to the transcendent and perfect *idea* alone—idea of beauty, of dignity, of comprehensive grace" (498). Yet James refuses to rest here—the "idea" is not enough. Speeding along in the "chariot of fire" as he calls it, he decides that Italy's "supreme heroic grace" is "the incomparable wrought *fusion,* fusion of human history and mortal passion with the elements of earth and air, of colour, composition and form" (502). And he recalls one particular element of this "congruous whole":

> the image of one of those human figures on which our perception of the romantic so often pounces in Italy as on the genius of the

> scene personified . . . a stalwart young gamekeeper, or perhaps
> substantial young farmer, who, well-appointed and blooming, had
> unslung his gun and resting on it beside a hedge, just lived for us,
> in the rare felicity of his whole look, during that moment. . . . He
> pointed, as it were, the lesson, giving the supreme right accent or
> final exquisite turn to the immense magnificent phrase; which from
> those moments on, and on and on, resembled doubtless nothing
> so much as a page written, by a consummate verbal economist and
> master of style, in the noblest of all tongues. (503–4)

This passage involves a "fusion" of its own: the "stalwart young
gamekeeper" becomes "the lesson" taught by a "master of style"
who is James himself.

This final clue to the nature of James's long love affair with
"the subtlest daughter of History" (498) makes it clear that he
has always been less stimulated by the "idea" of Italy than by the
"fusion" Italy comprises. Behind the romance he has always
sought the reality; what has interested him and still interests him
most is not Italy's tendency to inspire irresponsible imaginings
but its capacity to reconcile diverse experience. *Italian Hours* ends
with a stop at Velletri that typically impresses him all out of
proportion to its outward significance:

> we stayed no long time, and "went to see" nothing; yet we com-
> municated to intensity, we lay at our ease in the bosom of the past,
> we practiced intimacy, in short, an intimacy so much greater than
> the mere accidental and ostensible; the difficulty for the right and
> grateful expression of which makes the old, the familiar tax on the
> luxury of loving Italy. (505)

In dealing with the Italian emotion James is to the last enchanted,
scrupulous and troubled; yet surely he had stayed long enough
to find the "right and grateful expression," surely he paid that
particular "tax" in full.

6

Epilogue
1914

Less than three years before his death Henry James referred to "the early glimpse of the blest old Italy" as "a privilege of the highest intensity." [1] His own glimpses began in 1869 and continued to 1907. What, in the end, did that "privilege" mean to him and to us who read him? First of all, it appears that more than any other, the experience of Italy revealed and enriched the underlying polarity of his creative urge, which on the one hand moved him to imagine, idealize, and romanticize, and at the other extreme to notate, specify, and depict social and ethical realities. Given these alternatives, what especially haunted and beguiled him about Italy was that its appeal seemed not only immune to moral judgment but even a result of that immunity. He always insisted on judging England, France and America morally, as exponents of civilized values and wielders of power whether intellectual or political; Italy, in contrast, represented only aesthetic values, and expounded nothing beyond the lovely and melancholy play of time over beauty and the flesh. [2]

This "sensuous pessimism," James felt, was at best pragmatic and at worst merely tempting, for he could never completely accept the life of the senses as its own justification, and persistently sought to balance it against some ethical counterpart, as Maggie and the Prince balance each other in *The Golden Bowl.* But the converse is also true. A man of James's background and temperament all too readily ranks the punctilious over the instinctive, the contemplative over the passionate, the spiritual over the sensual; Europe in general helped deflect this bias and Italy in particular challenged it directly as the triumphant embodied alternative to his puritan predispositions. The effect of Italy on him was finally paradoxical: it meant romance and the dangers of romance and the sensual realities beneath romance, alternately and also simultaneously. This paradox was surely part of its "incomparable wrought fusion," and a major reason for James's perennially renewed fascination with "the blest old Italy."

NOTES

I. PROLOGUE: 1869

1. Henry James, *The Selected Letters of Henry James,* ed. Leon Edel (New York: Farrar, Straus and Cudahy, 1955), p. 28.

2. Henry James, *The Art of Travel,* ed. Morton Dauwen Zabel (Garden City, N. Y.: Doubleday, 1958), p. 313. Zabel earlier remarks that "in no other country did James find his spirit so freed of confinement, of fixed and conscious identity; so liberated from practical personal decision and responsibility. . . . It was Italy that give his fiction its moments of deepest resonance, his drama and tragedy their most memorable images of knowledge, recognition, and justice" (p. 44).

3. The comment appears in "Benvolio" (1875), one of James's most unusual early works: see *The Complete Tales of Henry James,* ed. Leon Edel, 12 vols. (London: Rupert Hart-Davis, 1961–64), III, 391; see also below, 3, II. I have consistently used this edition of James's shorter fiction, which is hereafter cited as *Complete Tales.* Edel's texts are those of either first book or original magazine publication; and in discussing James's novels before *The Ambassadors,* I have referred to the earliest book texts available.

4. Leon Edel, *Henry James, The Untried Years: 1843–1870* (Philadelphia: Lippincott, 1953), p. 301.

5. *Selected Letters,* p. 30. Dickens entitled his Venetian chapter in *Pictures from Italy* (1846) "An Italian Dream."

6. *The Untried Years,* p. 303.

7. Henry James, *The Letters of Henry James,* ed. Percy Lubbock, 2 vols. (London: Macmillan, 1920), I, 24–5.

8. Henry James, *Literary Reviews and Essays on American, English and French Literature,* ed. Albert Mordell (New York: Twayne, 1957), pp. 199–200.

9. William Dean Howells, *Italian Journeys* (New York, 1867), p. 87.

10. *Childe Harold's Pilgrimage,* Canto IV, st. xxvi. Byron's outburst recalls Goethe's famous yearning for "das Land, wo die Zitronen blühn" in the poem opening Book III of *Wilhelm Meisters Lehrjahre.*

11. For a more extended consideration of Story, see below, 5, II.

12. *The Untried Years,* p. 300.

13. A more thorough listing of James's many fictional references to Italy is furnished by Nathalia Wright in *American Novelists in Italy, The Discoverers: Allston to James* (Philadelphia: University of Pennsylvania Press, 1965), pp. 198–248. Wright believes that "the influence of Italy on James's fiction was pervasive" (p. 217).

14. *Italian Journeys,* p. 157. See also Van Wyck Brooks, *The Dream of Arcadia: American Writers and Artists in Italy 1760–1915* (New York: Dutton, 1958), p. 176: "the fall of papal Rome and the unification of Italy were the death-blow of mediaevalism, together with romantic Italy and the picturesque."

15. *Italian Journeys,* p. 138; *Letters,* I, 23.

16. Henry James, *The Scenic Art,* ed. Allan Wade (New Brunswick, N.J.: Rutgers University Press, 1948), p. 188. James is commenting, in 1884, on Salvini's acting, which he finds characteristic of "the Italian imagination."

17. Henry James, *The Golden Bowl* (New York, 1908), I, 198.

II. A MORAL HOLIDAY: 1869–1873

1. *The Untried Years,* pp. 334–5.

2. Bruce R. McElderry Jr., *Henry James* (New York: Twayne, 1965), p. 31; and cf. the verbally parallel evocations of St. Peter's in *Complete Tales,* II, 221 and *Letters,* I, 25.

3. *Complete Tales,* II, 179. All subsequent references will be included in the text.

4. It is interesting, however, to read of this story that James "succeeds in writing a spontaneous, effortless, flowing style . . . in comparing this style with that of the American tales of the previous four years, one feels that [he] has arrived at a much happier medium of expression for subject matter far more in keeping with his real interests and talent" (Robert

C. Le Clair, *Young Henry James* [New York: Bookman Associates, 1955], p. 435).

5. Henry James, *The Art of the Novel: Critical Prefaces,* introd. R. P. Blackmur (New York: Charles Scribner's Sons, 1934), p. 34.

6. James Russell Lowell, "Leaves from my Journal in Italy and Elsewhere," *The Writings of James Russell Lowell* (Boston, 1893), I, 125. Lowell and James were good friends from 1872 until the former's death in 1891.

7. James seems to have been greatly struck by Tintoretto's genius for reconciling extremes: see below, 2, IV.

8. The usual discrimination is of course between profane lust for the material and sacred contemplation of the spititual; James very nearly reverses this commonplace.

9. Cf. 1, I above and Goethe's hyperbolic tribute: "Wenn ich bei meiner Ankunft in Italien wie neu geboren war, so fange ich jetzt an wie neu erzogen sein." See *Italienische Reise,* "Dritter Teil," under December 21, 1787.

10. *Complete Tales,* II, 307. All subsequent references will be included in the text. Edith Wharton (*Italian Backgrounds,* New York, 1905, p. 3) similarly speaks of a transition "from the region of the obviously picturesque to that sophisticated landscape where the face of nature seems moulded by the passions and imaginings of man."

11. McElderry, *Henry James,* p. 31.

12. According to Cornelia Pulsifer Kelley (*The Early Development of Henry James* [Urbana: University of Illinois Press, 1965], p. 115), "At Isella" depicts "the land . . . not of art, not of convention, but of passion, the Italy discovered to James by Stendhal."

13. Henry James, Jr., *Transatlantic Sketches* (Boston, 1875), p. 73. All subsequent references are to this edition and will be included in the text.

14. Howells (*Italian Journeys,* pp. 287–8) mentions reaching "a bend in the lake, and all the roofs and towers of the city of Como pass from view, as if they had been so much architecture painted on a scene and shifted out of sight at a theatre."

15. Before "Daisy Miller" (1878), only "A Light Man" (1869), "Madame de Mauves" (1874), and "Four Meetings" (1877) seem to me of comparable quality.

16. *Complete Tales,* III, 14–15. All subsequent references will be included in the text.

17. This same idea occurs in Balzac's curious "Massimilla Doni" (1839), *La Comédie Humaine* (Paris, Editions Louis Conard, 1954), xxvii, 448: "Raphaël seul a réuni la Forme et l'Idée." It was perhaps a contemporary cliché.

18. *Transatlantic Sketches,* pp. 91–2; and see above, p. 16.

19. See Madame de Staël, whose Corinne admits that Italians are inclined to "flatterie" but insists that "le plupart du temps ce n'est point par le calcul, mais seulement par desir de plaire, qu'ils prodiguent leurs douces expressions" (Bk. VI, ch. 4).

20. It is hinted that the mentality responsible for such art is also debased: Serafina's lover seems to the narrator "little more than an exceptionally intelligent ape" (45).

21. *Transatlantic Sketches,* p. 116. All subsequent references will be included in the text.

22. As has been often noted, James based his story on Merimée's "La Venus d'Ille" (1837); the change from Venus to Juno perhaps indicates an emphasis on the past as a coherent alternative to the present rather than just a dark primal force impinging on it.

23. Leon Edel, *Henry James, The Conquest of London: 1870–1881* (Philadelphia: Lippincott, 1962), p. 102.

24. See the entry in *The French and Italian Notebooks* for May 29, 1859, where Hawthorne also gives full expression to his extremely mixed feelings about Rome.

25. *Complete Tales,* III, 107. All subsequent references will be included in the text.

26. It is a measure of James's artistic development that while Conte Valerio is directly and rather ironically compared to a statue, Amerigo's "artificiality" is more subtly established by associating him with representative precious objects like the golden bowl itself.

27. Cf. Prince Amerigo below, 5, III.

28. *Complete Tales,* III, 257. All subsequent references will be included in the text.

29. The initial encounter with Angelo seems directly inspired by an actual occurrence recorded in the "Roman Rides" section of *Transatlantic Sketches* (pp. 153–4).

30. For example, in *Roderick Hudson* (ch. XIII) and in "Daisy Miller."

31. Madame de Staël speaks of love in Italy as "une impression

rapide et profonde, qui s'exprimeroit bien plutôt par des actions silencieuses et passionées que par un ingenieux langage" (*Corinne*, Bk. VII, ch. ii).

32. *Literary Reviews and Essays*, p. 156.

III. THE ITALIAN EMOTION: 1874–1881

1. *Transatlantic Sketches*, p. 287. All subsequent references will be included in the text.

2. *The Art of the Novel*, p. 3. James purposely ignores the puerile *Watch and Ward* (1871).

3. F. W. Dupee, *Henry James* (Garden City, N. Y.: Doubleday, 1956), p. 74.

4. Henry James, *Roderick Hudson* (Boston, 1876), p. 29. All subsequent references are to this edition and will be included in the text.

5. Cf. The "Platonism" of "At Isella," *Complete Tales*, II, 327–8.

6. Henry James, *Roderick Hudson* (New York, 1908), p. 201.

7. *The Art of the Novel*, pp. 6–7.

8. Cf. James on William Wetmore Story, below, 5, II. There is reason to believe that Rowland's tense delight in the Italian ambiance was also James's own, e.g., the comment on how Rome "enforced a sort of oppressive reconciliation" was thus revised four years later: "it brought with it a relaxed acceptance of the present" (*Roderick Hudson* [Boston and New York, 1882], p. 115; the text reproduces the first English edition of 1879). This near *volte-face* perhaps indicates growing sophistication, or continued uncertainty, or both.

9. James also made more complex alterations, for instance in a sentence describing Roderick's quarters in Rome, "The place was crumbling and shabby and melancholy, but the river was delightful, the rent a trifle, and every thing picturesque." He later replaced "melancholy" with "sinister" and "picturesque" with "romantic" (*1875*, p. 68; *1908*, p. 78): the second version sharpens the implications of the first into perceptible irony.

10. Cristina Giorcelli, in an interesting study of *Henry James e l'Italia* (Roma: Edizioni di Storia e Letteratura, 1968), deals with several facets of the subject that lie outside the scope of this present inquiry, e.g., she offers a full and sympathetic account of the Cavaliere Giacosa (p. 131).

11. It is odd that only characters from James's "Italian" stories appear again after long intervals; see also 4, VIII below.

12. See below, 4, VII.

13. Dupee, *Henry James*, p. 133.

14. *The Conquest of London*, p. 179.

15. *Complete Tales*, III, 358. "Casa massima" roughly translated is "great house."

16. Henry James, *Portraits of Places* (Boston, 1884), p. 42. All subsequent references are to this edition and will be included in the text.

17. Howells on the other hand (*Italian Journeys*, p. 152) thought modern Italy "hideous"; James for once seems the less aesthetically oriented of the two.

18. The young Italian "communist" distinctly foreshadows the political bohemians and alienated radicals that James treated nine years later in *The Princess Casamassima*. Giorcelli nevertheless maintains that "James non volle mai impegnarsi in alcun modo nella realtà italiana" (p. 150), a statement true enough to merit qualification.

19. *The Art of the Novel*, p. 268.

20. *Complete Tales*, IV, 201. All subsequent references will be included in the text.

21. *Childe Harold's Pilgrimage*, Canto IV, st. cxxx.

22. See below, 4, VIII.

23. Henry James, " 'Very Modern Rome'—An Unpublished Essay of Henry James," *Harvard Library Bulletin*, VIII (Spring 1954), 136.

24. *Complete Tales*, IV, 389. All subsequent references will be included in the text.

25. Interestingly enough, John Marcher and May Bartram of "The Beast in the Jungle" recall how they originally met in Naples: see *Complete Tales*, XI, pp. 354–7.

26. Ibid., III, 42.

27. *Portraits of Places*, p. 8. All subsequent references will be included in the text. See also *Letters*, I, 386.

28. Madame de Staël (*Corinne*, Bk. XV, ch. viii) similarly finds that "le dialecte venetien est doux et lèger comme un souffle agréable," and refers to "ces sons delicats et presque enfantins."

29. Years later James recalled how at this juncture he discovered that "romantic and historic sites, such as the land of Italy abounds in, offer

the artist a questionable aid to concentration when they themselves are not to be the subject of it": *The Art of the Novel*, p. 40, and see below, 5, II.

30. *Letters*, I, 36. James met the critic Enrico Nencioni in 1887 and Mathilde Serao in 1890; his only close "Italian" friend was Count Giuseppe Primoli (Ibid., I, 246; Giorcelli, pp. 102, 153).

31. *Literary Reviews and Essays*, pp. 203–4. James is reviewing Howells's *A Foregone Conclusion*. The priest Don Ippolito in this novel perhaps represents, as a distinctly atypical Italian, the very type that James despaired of ever being able to create.

32. Henry James, *Hawthorne* (London, 1879), pp. 159, 166.

33. *Henry James e l'Italia*, p. 119.

34. Henry James Jr., *The Portrait of a Lady* (Boston, 1882), p. 394. All subsequent references are to this first edition and will be included in the text.

35. The revision of this passage in the New York Edition (1908) triumphantly suggests the venal underside of Osmond's aestheticism: he is compared to a "fine gold coin," or rather an "elegant complicated medal struck off for a special occasion" (I, 329).

36. The quoted passages are from Chapter 20, paragraphs 4 and 5.

IV. DEATHS IN VENICE: 1882–1902

1. Leon Edel, *Henry James, The Middle Years: 1882–1895* (Philadelphia: Lippincott, 1962), p. 85.

2. *Letters*, I, 106. A month later James learns that Mrs. Symonds "was in no sort of sympathy with what [her husband] wrote," and sees possibilities "in the opposition between the narrow, cold, Calvinistic wife, a rigid moralist; and the husband, impregnated—even to morbidness—with the spirit of Italy, the love of beauty, of art, the aesthetic view of life" (*The Notebooks of Henry James*, ed. F. O. Matthiessen and Kenneth B. Murdock [New York: George Braziller, 1955], p. 57). He made immediate use of this donnée in "The Author of Beltraffio" (1884), where "the spirit of Italy" permeates an English setting with the faint, spicy aroma of exquisite amorality.

3. *Complete Tales*, VI, 45, 72, 79; and *Daniel Deronda* (1876) and *He Knew He Was Right* (1868), respectively.

4. Henry James, *The Princess Casamassima* (London, 1886), p. 377. All subsequent references are to this edition and will be included in the text.

5. Hyacinth is thus the mirror-image of the young Italian radical James met near Genoa; see above, 3, III.

6. *The Art of the Novel*, pp. 73–4.

7. *Roderick Hudson* (1882), p. 268. In 1876 the second word was "corruptible"—James's passion for revision began early.

8. *The Art of the Novel*, p. 74.

9. *Letters*, I, 126.

10. Giorcelli (*Henry James e l'Italia*, pp. 39–45) attempts to differentiate the varying functions these three cities perform in Jamesian fiction.

11. Byron writes in the Preface to *Marino Faliero:* "Everything about Venice is, or was, extraordinary—her aspect is like a dream and her history is like a romance."

12. *Complete Tales*, VI, 305. All subsequent references will be included in the text.

13. When James revised this tale for the New York Edition he changed "Tita" into the more euphonious "Tina."

14. *The Art of the Novel*, p. 164.

15. *Complete Tales*, VII, 351. All subsequent references will be included in the text.

16. One is oddly reminded of Miss Tita in "The Aspern Papers" mourning the long-passed era when she and her aunt had lovely English friends, "the Churtons and the *Goldies* and Mrs. Stock-Stock" (*Complete Tales*, VI, 317—italics mine).

17. This impetus was largely lost when James converted "The Solution" into a play called *Disengaged* (1892). The action was transferred to England and the names of the characters changed; though the story retains a certain charm, the play is a frantic wilderness of monkeyshines.

18. *Letters*, I, 194.

19. See *The Middle Years*, pp. 348–89 passim.

20. Leon Edel, *Henry James, The Treacherous Years: 1895–1901* (Philadelphia: Lippincott, 1969), p. 313; see also pp. 306–16 passim. Later James had similar relationships with Jocelyn Persse and Hugh Walpole.

21. Henry James, "The Grand Canal," *Scribner's Magazine*, XII (Nov.

1892), 531. All subsequent references are to this volume and will be included in the text.

22. Henry James, *Italian Hours* (New York: Horizon Press, 1968), p. 89. All subsequent references are to this edition and will be included in the text.

23. Mrs. Humphry Ward, *A Writer's Recollections,* 2 vols. (New York: Harper & Brothers, 1918), II, 195; see also 195–201 passim, and *The Treacherous Years,* p. 294.

24. James was commissioned to write the biography in 1897, two years after Story's death. See *Selected Letters,* p. 100.

25. *Complete Tales,* IX, 99. All subsequent references will be included in the text.

26. *Notebooks,* p. 189.

27. Ibid., pp. 226, 227.

28. Henry James, *The Ambassadors* (New York, 1908), I, 217. All subsequent references are to this volume of this edition and will be included in the text.

29. *The Art of the Novel,* p. 74.

30. *Roderick Hudson* (1875), p. 74; Eliot's brief essay is reprinted in *The Question of Henry James,* ed. F. W. Dupee (New York: Henry Holt, 1945), p. 110.

31. *Complete Tales,* XII, 238. All subsequent references will be included in the text.

32. James just possibly did not intend us to think of the two Eugenios as the same person; but mere inadvertence seems unlikely considering the importance of "Daisy Miller" in his career.

33. Henry James, *The Wings of the Dove* (New York, 1908), II, 132. All subsequent references are to this volume of this edition and will be included in the text.

34. Frederick C. Crews, *The Tragedy of Manners* (New Haven: Yale University Press, 1957), p. 66; see also p. 68: "Milly's tragedy is that she cannot escape the romantic appeal of her situation."

35. J. A. Ward, *The Imagination of Disaster* (Lincoln: University of Nebraska Press, 1951), p. 129.

36. Giorcelli comments (*Henry James e l'Italia,* p. 53) that Densher "fa veramente del paesaggio una mera proiezione del suo stato d'animo."

37. Henry James, "Browning in Venice. Being recollections by the late Katharine De Kay Bronson, with a prefatory note by Henry James," *Cornhill Magazine,* XII (Feb. 1902), 14.

V. A CONGRUOUS WHOLE: 1903–1909

1. *Italian Hours,* pp. 484–6, 495. All subsequent references will be included in the text.
2. See above, 4, IV.
3. Henry James, *Notes on Novelists with Some Other Notes* (New York, 1914), pp. 245, 300. All subsequent references are to this edition and will be included in the text.
4. The cartoon is reproduced in *The Treacherous Years,* p. 360; see also S. N. Behrman, *Portrait of Max* (New York: Random House, 1960), pp. 246–7.
5. *Letters,* I, 413.
6. Unpublished MS letter to Mrs. Story dated June 14, 1903, in the Humanities Research Center Library of the University of Texas at Austin.
7. *Letters,* I, 246. James writes to Mrs. Gardner, March 23, 1895: "I rejoice with you in *your* Rome—but my Rome is in the buried past."
8. Henry James, *William Wetmore Story and His Friends from letters, diaries, and recollections,* 2 vols. (Boston, 1903), I, 245. All subsequent references are to this edition and will be included in the text.
9. *Letters,* I, 420.
10. MS letter of June 14, 1903, at the University of Texas.
11. *Letters,* I, 413.
12. The poem dates from 1857 and ends the definitive version of *Émaux et Camées.* See James's enthusiastic account of Gautier written in 1874, *Literary Reviews and Essays,* pp. 94–103.
13. Though he foresaw the danger as early as 1877, when he spoke of how "the old enchantment of Rome . . . becomes really almost a nuisance and an importunity. That is, it keeps you from working, from staying indoors, etc. To do those things in sufficient measure one must live in an ugly country . . ." *Letters,* I, 57.
14. James must have found composing *William Wetmore Story* excessively difficult, since over a decade after its publication he wrote to Mrs.

Waldo Story to lament, "for the relief of my own spirit," the "extremely embarrassing scantness and futility" of the Story memorabilia: "I was thrown back altogether on a desperate ingenuity, . . . the book coming into existence, on my part, by a real miracle of art and tact and literary resource. . . . If I hadn't been able to kick up, by the aid of my own imagination and reminiscence, by that in short, as I say, of my own zealous ingenuity, a certain amount of vague Roman gold-dust and make it hover over the scene, the book could never have existed at all." MS letter of March 28, 1914, at the University of Texas.

15. *Notebooks*, p. 131.

16. Dupee, *Henry James*, p. 225.

17. Henry James, *The Golden Bowl*, 2 vols. (New York, 1908), I, 12. All subsequent references are to this edition and will be included in the text.

18. *The Complete Plays of Henry James*, ed. Leon Edel (London: Rupert Hart-Davis, 1949), p. 705. The heroine is Rose Armiger of *The Other House* (1896).

19. Dorothea Krook, *The Ordeal of Consciousness in Henry James* (Cambridge: Cambridge University Press, 1962), p. 309, speaks of Charlotte's "redemption by pride": i.e., another supreme irony in this supremely ironic novel is that the cause of her downfall is also what enables her to survive it.

20. It can be and has been seriously maintained that Amerigo changes too; I prefer to believe that we simply understand him more fully by the end of the novel.

21. See for example II, 21, 109, 117, 172, 234, 239, 278, 310.

22. Giorcelli (*Henry James e l'Italia*, p. 138) calls Amerigo "la realizzazione più sofisticata del tipo umano che James riconosceva e vedeva in ogni italiano."

23. Its only possible rival is the description of the kiss that Caspar Goodwood bestows on Isabel Archer at the end of *Portrait of a Lady*. The original version is notably tame—"His kiss was like a flash of lightning; when it was dark again she was free"—and all the passage's intensity derives from its post-*Golden Bowl* revision: cf. *1882*, p. 519; *1908*, II, 436; see also the vividly carnal letter of 1906 to Hendrik Anderson quoted in Leon Edel, *Henry James, The Master: 1901–1916* (Philadelphia: Lippincott, 1972), p. 470.

24. See above, 2, I. Gold figures prominently in the earlier story too.

25. Christof Wegelin, *The Image of Europe in Henry James* (Dallas: Southern Methodist University Press, 1958), p. 129.

26. *Letters*, II, 80; see also *The Master*, pp. 346–51.

27. *Italian Hours*, p. 303. All subsequent references will be included in the text. The new material in *Italian Hours* is: "A Few Other Roman Neighbourhoods," "Siena Early and Late" (Part II), "Other Tuscan Cities," and "The Saint's Afternoon and Others" (Parts VI and VII). The revisions of older material are often very interesting: for example, in 1881 James sees the Italians as "peculiarly susceptible to the tender sentiment" (*Portraits of Places*, p. 20), in 1909 as "loving if not too well at least too often" (p. 23)!

28. The phrase also occurs in a letter to Edmund Gosse of Feb. 16, 1905 (*Letters*, II, 25), and perhaps figures elsewhere in James's later writings.

29. Ibid., II, 77.

VI. EPILOGUE: 1914

1. Henry James, *Notes of a Son and Brother* (New York, 1914), p. 39.

2. James's friend Henry Adams formulates this response with typical astringency in ch. VI of his *Education:* "To a young Bostonian, fresh from Germany, Rome seemed a pure emotion, quite free from economic or actual values. . . ."

Index